all about creative textiles

Stephanie K Holland

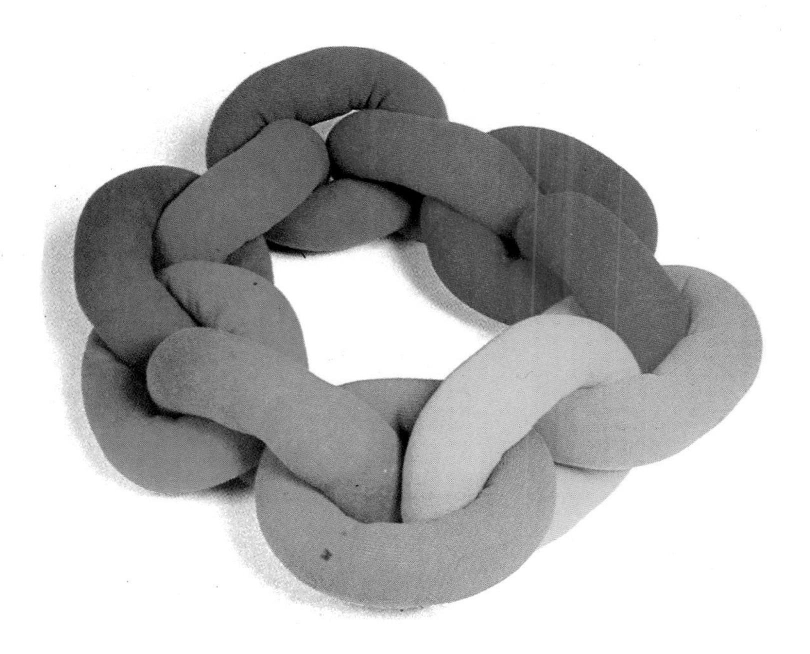

Oxford University Press

Oxford University Press, Walton Street, Oxford OX2 6DP

Oxford New York Toronto
Delhi Bombay Calcutta Madras Karachi
Petaling Jaya Singapore Hong Kong Tokyo
Nairobi Dar es Salaam Cape Town
Melbourne Auckland

and associated companies in
Berlin Ibadan

Reprinted 1988 (twice)
ISBN 0 19 832737 4

Acknowledgements

The illustrations are by Sheelagh Bowie, Alan Rowe, Mike Saunders and Jacqui Thomas.

The publishers would like to thank the following for permission to reproduce photographs:

American Museum of Britain p.12; Crafts Council: Sutton/Treen FRONT COVER, R.Dymtrenko BACK COVER, A.Sutton p.1, P.Burbridge p.8 (bottom), P.Russell p.44 (top), J.Bolton p.44 (bottom), M.Rogoyska p.53 (top), H.Yardley p.59, G.Sida p.77 (top left), A.Tilson p.77 (top right), G.Sida p.77 (bottom right); Rob Judges p.4, p.5, p.8 (middle), p.9, p.11 (right), p.33, p.34, p.36, p.37, p.40, p.41, p.46, p.47, p.48, p.49, p.51 (left and middle), p.53 (bottom), p.56, p.61, p.62, p.63, p.68, p.70, p.71, p.72 (right), p.75, p.77 (bottom left); Dudley Moss p.72 (left), p.73; Oxford Scientific Films Picture Library: Doug Allan p.8 (top), Barrie Watts p.11 (left); Derek Widdicombe p.10.

The publishers would like to thank the following for permission to reproduce their work:

Banbury School: Sue Moore and pupils; Rachel Burdon p.11 (right), Joanne Collins p.48, Rebecca Lester p.49; Chipping Norton School: William Jefferies and pupils p.5 (bottom left), p.53 (bottom); Helen Fairfield p.51 (right); Stephanie Holland p.8 (middle), p.33, p.34, p.40, p.41, p.46, p.47, p.51 (left and middle), p.56, p.61, p.62, p.63, p.68, p.70, p.71; Mr Holland p.9 (top); Shelley Lazar p.72 (right); Oxford College of Further Education: Jane Hillman and pupils p.9 (bottom), p.36, p.37, Judith Peterson p.75.

The author would like to thank her father E.C.Holland for his contributions to the book, and for typing the manuscript.

Phototypeset by Tradespools Limited, Frome, Somerset
Printed in Hong Kong

Contents

All about creative textiles

The study of creative textiles ranges from embroidery to soft sculpture to tie-and-dye to almost any use of fabric. Here are some examples of work from school students which will inspire you to begin working creatively with textiles.

All of these 'beachscapes' are by Sharon Plaice of Banbury School

Fabric-painted wall hanging by Phillip Sutton of Banbury School

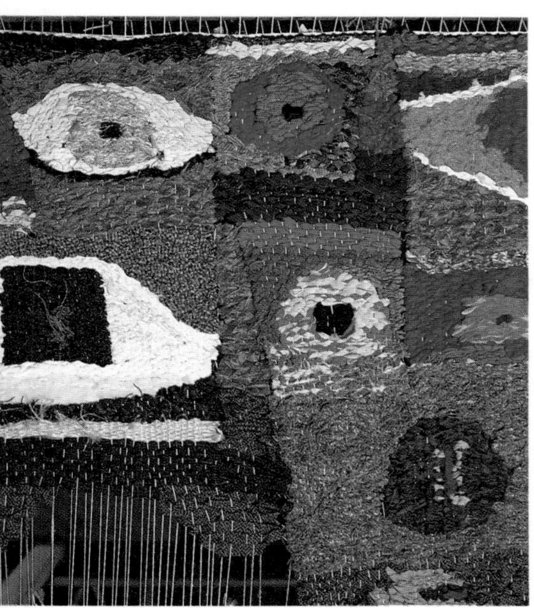

'Woven eyes' by the fourth form at Chipping Norton Comprehensive School

'A cottage garden' by Louise Mills of Banbury School

'Fruity cushions' by the third form at Wantage Comprehensive School

Introduction

All about creative textiles is a guide to working creatively from a brief.
The book is in three parts bringing together creativity, mastery of design problems, and techniques.

Part 1 deals with the principles of design,
Part 2 deals with construction techniques,
Part 3 shows how design briefs can be realized, giving examples of both worked and unworked briefs.

The problem

All aspects of creative work involve problem-solving. In order to reach the *right* solution, the problem needs to be considered from every angle. Consider the problem of making an item:

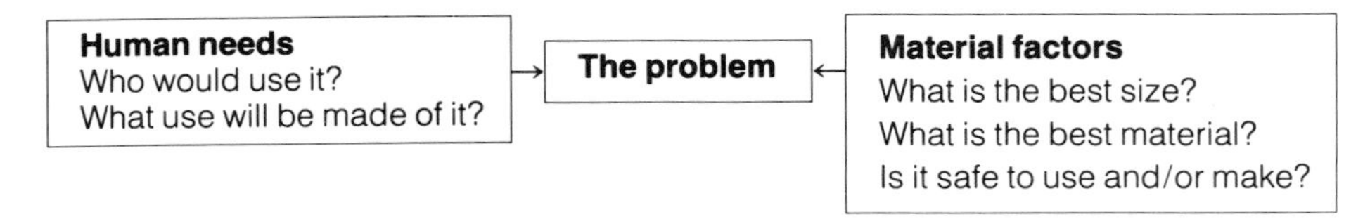

Human needs

Material factors have to meet human needs, so we start by thinking about who the item is for.
What factors do we need to take into account?

Age
The age of the user affects the size of the item, whether it is for wearing or for handling. It is not just the age in years but the stage in physical development that should be considered. A large teddybear may appeal to teenagers but an infant will find a small soft toy easier to play with.

It is important to consider what the child can do, particularly when choosing fastenings. Can the toy be a learning-aid too? Some items, however, are specifically designed to prevent children using them. Can you name some? Why are they so designed?

Other changes occur with age as well as physical development. Do you do the same things now as you did two years ago? Are your views the same about clothing, boys/girls, music, games, hair styles. . . ? Personal taste must be considered when making a design decision.

Physical state
Sometimes the physical condition of the user can put restrictions on a design. A game designed for a child lying flat in hospital might be very different from a game designed for a healthy child. Similarly, fastenings on clothes or on a bag for an elderly person with arthritic hands would also need special thought.

Aesthetic appeal
One very important factor is that whatever we create should look as attractive as possible. We are all happier to use, wear, or look at something more often, if it is pleasing to the eye. This is called aesthetic appeal. It explains why we decorate things. In creative work we consider it at every stage.

Material factors

By first establishing the human needs of the design we can identify the qualities required from the materials to be used. We then try to match them with the textiles available to us. At this stage it is important to research and investigate textiles and shapes, to see what will fulfil the needs outlined. One factor which is sometimes overlooked is how a fabric will react to its surroundings. Faded curtains, a mildewed picture, or a burned hearthrug, can be avoided by careful choice of a material that can cope with its environment. Careful evaluation (judging) of materials and designs helps to ensure the item's success in use.

Efficiency

The quickest and best method of making something can be worked out in advance too, by looking at what has to be done and matching techniques with the fabric, the time available, and the designer's ability.

It is extremely important to make a final evaluation after completing and using the item. It may justify what you have done, and you can learn by your mistakes.

Recording

It is essential to keep a file containing details of each piece of work completed. The file should contain:

1 the brief
2 the research and investigations that formed the basis of the design
3 notes on how the design was transferred on to the material
4 the reasons for the choice of processes and order of work
5 the problems encountered
6 an evaluation – was the brief realized?

The file might also contain sources of inspiration, e.g. photographs, sketches, pieces of unusual material, etc.

The design file itself can also be a source of inspiration.

▲ Design an attractive cover for your file.

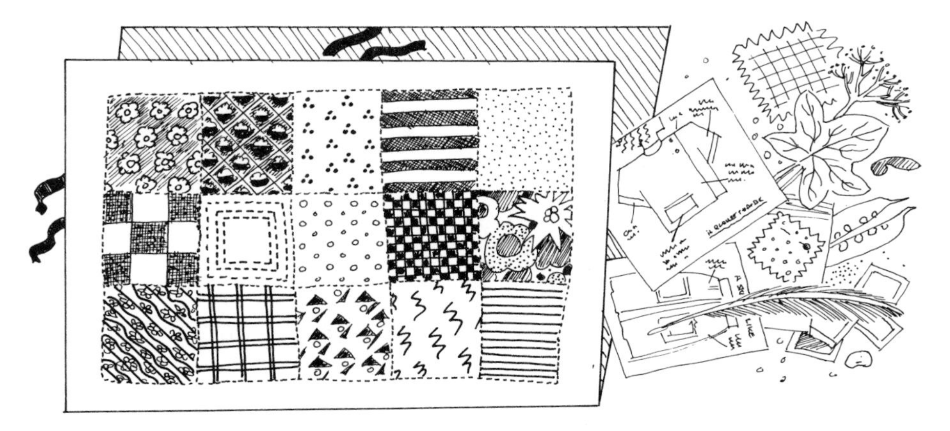

Creative textile work is an absorbing adventure, so start right at the beginning with finding designs.

Part 1

Finding designs

A spider's web ...

... makes a simple design ...

... or a more abstract one

Designs fall into three categories; **natural**, **abstract**, and **geometric**.

Natural designs

Ideas from nature

Natural lines, shapes, and colours can be interpreted in decorative textile work in several different ways.

Simple delicate lines lend themselves to fine embroidery or pin and thread work. Alternatively, a shape can be enlarged and used as a single decorative feature with striking effect.

Once we become aware of the shape of the natural things around us we begin to realize the enormous potential of simple lines, and of the many ways that they can be used in textile work.

Drawing round a leaf, shell, or feather, or sketching from nature produces a basic outline, and looking at illustrations in nature books can help when transferring the design to paper.

Some features can actually be incorporated into textile designs to provide texture and to give a third dimension (depth) or thickness to decorative work. For example using different materials and stitches to work an outline again and again achieves an interesting textured effect.

▲ Go into the garden and look for shapes which could be used in textile design. Draw them (with the help of a book if necessary). Then look through this book to see which medium the design might look best in.

▲ On a field walk collect items which could be used to provide interesting shapes and textures for a three-dimensional piece of work. You might find wool, hair, tree bark, feathers, etc.

▲ Even wasteland can be a design inspiration. Visit such an area and photograph or sketch ideas for your design file.

Ideas from materials

At home a number of everyday things provide different surfaces and textures which can be a design inspiration.

Wood is a good background for mounting textile work, but look more closely at the grain lines on it. The beautiful grains and colour of a variety of fine layers of wood, known as veneers, can be blended together to make a design.

Attractive effects can be achieved by varying **fabric textures**, e.g. coarse – hessian for background; sheer – tricel or acetate; diaphanous (see-through) for shadow work. Lint, felt, carpet scraps, corduroy, and sandpaper also provide different textures. Lentils, allspice berries, and millet grain can be used to create special effects.

Every material in the textile room can be a design inspiration

You can put the finishing touches to your article in many ways:

a wools and embroidery threads can be decorative features

b sparkly or coloured beads catch the eye

c studs, buttons, and trims finish off an article.

Questions

1 Look carefully at the wood picture above. For how many different items are the grain lines used? Make a list of the things that the grain lines of wood or similarly lined fabric might portray in a picture.

2 On tissue paper trace a section of the grain lines of a wooden table. Can you draw a simple picture using those lines?

Finding designs II

Ideas from books

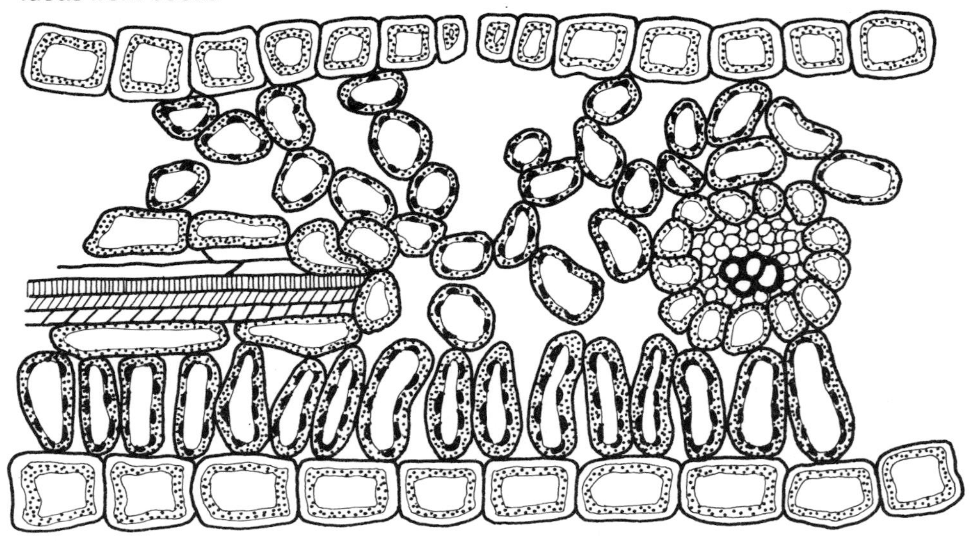

These leaf cells might be used as a basis for a textured design

History, geography, and biblical books feature figures in historical and foreign dress, tapestries, and heraldry.

Fairy stories have simple illustrations of appealing characters and animals from the world of make-believe.

Biology books show:

a drawings of snails, flowers, butterflies, and birds
b diagrams of cell structures through a microscope which give interesting and sometimes symmetrical lines.

Look for pictures or diagrams of man-made things such as wheels, street plans, buildings, windows, walls, etc. They suggest particular techniques in which they can be realized in textiles.

▲ Leaflets and magazines contain illustrations which can be used in textile work. Find some, stick them on to paper and suggest how you might use them.

▲ Produce a logo for your tracksuit using letters cut from newspaper headlines. Stick it on to graph paper ready to use later.

▲ Find and sketch an illustration of a Roman aqueduct, a wigwam, or a dam. Add them to your design file.

How many designs can you see here?

Abstract design

An abstract design does not portray its source (or inspiration) exactly. A natural design and an abstract one might use the same source, e.g. a leaf, but the results would be quite different. The natural design would be recognizable as a leaf whereas the abstract design would use the textures, veins, and patterns of sunlight and shade on the leaf to produce an attractive pattern.

Looking for patterns
Abstract design takes practice in looking for patterns. Everyday objects when viewed from different angles can be exciting design sources.

A photograph of lichen ...

... is embroidered as an abstract

- ▲ Look for patterns in the countryside, in the home (foods can be a good design source), in the classroom, and in the street. Keep a record of your ideas and put them in your file.
- ▲ Take an object, e.g. a piece of wood, and sketch a design from it that is not recognizable as the wood. How many different patterns can you make from it?

Doodling
Abstract designs often start from doodles.

- ▲ Start with a line or curve and keep adding to it until a pattern or shape appears. Try using this 'unit' of pattern to build up a complete design.

Ideas from the computer
Experiments in abstract design can be carried out using a computer program such as Mosaic RML 380Z (16 colours) or 480Z (8 colours) on disc or cassette.

Notice that because the colours come from light, the primary ones are red, green, and blue as in the rainbow, and not the primary colours from pigments (p.16).

Finished ideas can be transferred to the print-out, or to graph paper, or can be photographed. The design can then be used in fabric printing, knitting, weaving, needlepoint, beadwork, etc.

Finding designs III

Geometric designs

Mathematics plays a part in textile design! A shape which can be used for a petal, leaf, or an abstract design, can be formed by geometric means with a straight line and a pair of compasses. This is called **bisecting a line.**

Method
Draw a straight line. Set the compasses to any distance greater than half the length of the line. Describe (draw) an arc (a part of a circle) from each end, above and below the line. This forms the shape of a petal or leaf. Draw a straight line to join the points where the two arcs cross. This line cuts the original line in half and is at right-angles to it (perpendicular).

Geometric shapes
Geometric shapes are often used in creative design. **Regular** shapes can be drawn from a circle. Regular means that each side is equal (and because of that each angle within the shape is equal too).

All the regular geometric shapes feature in the following exercise about drawing polygons. A polygon is a many-sided shape.
You could use the diagram to trace from, but it is more useful if you understand how to construct your own shapes so that you can make them whatever size you wish, to be in proportion to the piece of work you do.

The use of dividers in geometrical design makes your work more accurate. You can set the distance between the two arms of the divider and use them to mark equal points on a line. By keeping one arm on one point you can swing the other round to make the next point. If you continue with this the line is divided into equal parts. This is known as **stepping off**.

This American patchwork quilt shows how effective geometric designs can be

The construction of a regular polygon
You will need: a sharp pencil, a pair of compasses, some dividers, and a set square.

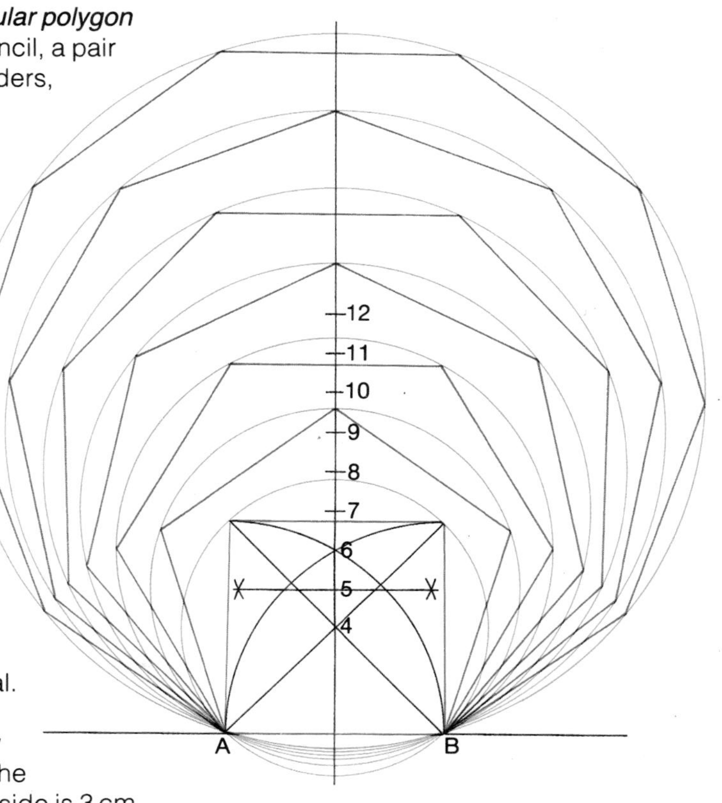

1 Draw a horizontal base line along the bottom of your page. Then, using the dividers, mark two points, **A** and **B**, 3 cm apart. The line **AB** will be one side of the polygon.

2 Bisect this line and draw a vertical line through it to the top of the page (the vertical).

3 Using the set square draw lines at 45° from **A** and **B** to cross the vertical. This gives us the centre point of the square. Draw the circle and complete the square; remember each side is 3 cm.

4 Now for the hexagon. Set the compasses to the length of the base line, and from each end of the baseline (**A** and **B**) draw arcs to cut the vertical. This gives us the centre point for the hexagon. Draw the circle. Using this radius step the sides round the circumference and complete the figure by 'joining the steps'.

5 Number these two centrepoints **4** for the square and **6** for the hexagon.

6 Bisect the distance between these two points and number this point **5** – the centre point for the pentagon.

7 Set the dividers to the distance between **5** and **6** (a unit distance) and step off up the vertical. Number the points as shown in the diagram.

8 More polygons can now be constructed by drawing the appropriate circle. The radius in each case will be from the number concerned to the end of the base line. Step off the length of the base line round the circumference. The steps are then joined to complete the figure. The construction can go on to any number of equal sides.

▲ Make geometrical templates of hexagons, triangles, diamonds, and squares. You can do this by cutting out the shapes you have made in stiff card. Geometrical shapes can be used to:

a make fabric collages (with glue) or appliqué
b reinforce or repair worn areas
c decorate clothes, cushions, satchels, or bags.

Space and proportion

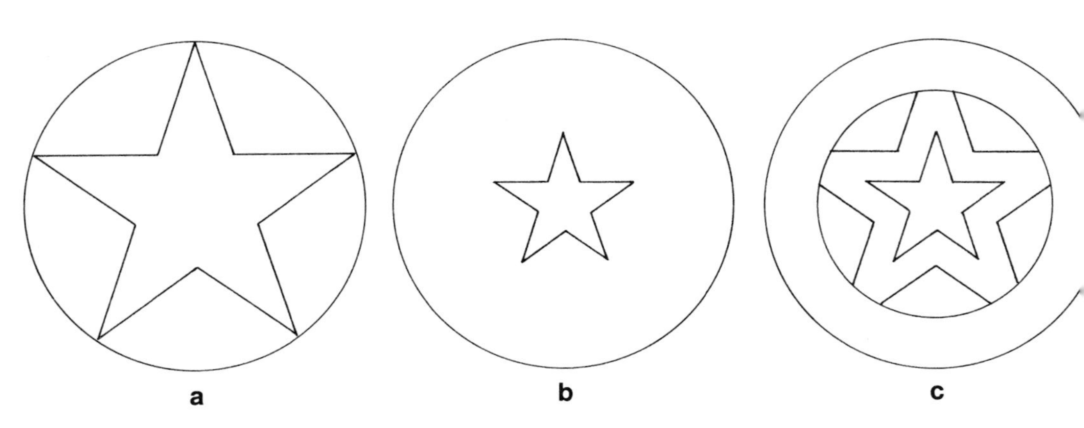

Look at the three designs above. Which of them looks odd and why? In **b** the star has not been drawn to the correct size in relation to the circle: it is not **in proportion** with the circle. In **a** the star and the circle *are* in proportion and would make a good design for e.g. a Christmas cake. To ensure a good design it is important to make use of all the available space and to keep the features of the design in proportion. In **c** new lines have been added to the star to fill the available space and to ensure that the design looks complete.

▲ Choose a picture from a magazine of a figure or animal approximately 5 cm × 3.5 cm. Cut round it. Place it on some blank sheets of paper of varying sizes from 5 cm^2 to 10 cm^2, A4, and drawing paper.
On what size of paper does the result look complete?

Experiment with the position of the figure to see where it looks best. Must it be in the centre? Can it be towards one side or the other? Could it be above or below the centre of the paper?

To look pleasing the design must be in proportion to the area on which it is used, so that it fills the space well. On a large piece of paper the figure could be used as *part* of a whole design, but it should include some background features.
Can you suggest other features which would fill the space? When the space is reasonably filled the picture looks finished.

Focal point

Sometimes designers want a particular figure in their design to catch the eye first. One way of achieving this is to surround the figure with blank space – pictures are sometimes framed with a white border for this reason. This figure is then known as a focal point.

▲ Experiment with a postcard-sized print and an A3 piece of blank paper. Stick your sheet of paper on to a wall with blu-tack and find the best position for the print to be stuck on it. Try the same experiment with a full-size print and a blank wall.

To achieve the best effect on a wall the print should be slightly above the centre of the paper with a proportional white area around it.

Why do you think this is so?

Blank space

A blank area looks larger than a covered one and sometimes use is made of this fact to give the feeling of spaciousness and size. A focal point is sometimes added for decorative interest.

Comic characters painted in the top corner of a plain, light-coloured bedroom wall make an attractive nursery feature, yet do not detract from the spacious feeling the plain light walls create.

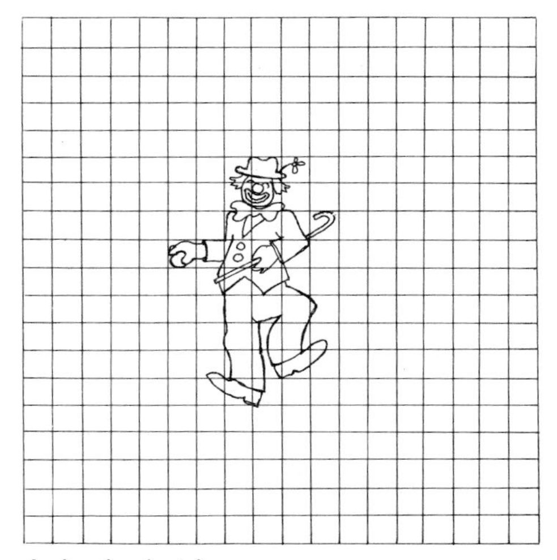

A simple sketch ...

Keeping in proportion

If you find drawing difficult, you can enlarge a design to the size you want using squared paper to keep the drawing in the right proportion.

Method

1. Find an illustration that you would like to use in a creative design.
2. Trace it using greaseproof paper.
3. Carbon the tracing on to graph paper.
4. Using the squares as a guide, draw the illustration on to larger squares.

By following the position of the outline on the squares, the drawing stays in proportion; i.e. each part is increased by the same amount in width and height, because the squares are the same shape but larger.

... is enlarged on squared paper

Proportion is extremely important in making drawings look realistic. An artist or painter uses proportion to capture reality on paper or canvas.

Squares have a further use – in the appropriate size they can represent cross-stitches, stitches in knitting or needle-point, cross beads in beadwork, or knots in rug making. By shading in the colours you want to use you can complete the working drawing for your design.

Colour

Light

White light or daylight is composed of different colours which we normally cannot see. When light passes through water the coloured light rays bend at different angles. Red bends the least and violet the most, with all the other colours ranged between. This separates the colours, and they become visible to the human eye, in order, as the seven colours of the rainbow. This bending of sunlight as it goes through raindrops, or through a prism, is called **refraction**.

In the rainbow red, green, and blue/violet are known as the **primary light colours** because together they make white light.

▲ You can experiment by shining light through coloured filters onto a white wall. Red, green, and blue circles dance individually on the wall, but when they all focus on the same spot white light is produced. Notice how all the other colours in light can be produced by mixing the primary ones.

Pigments

The colours in the paintbox and, most importantly, the ones used in textiles come from pigments. Pigment colours *look* the same as light colours but *behave* differently.

Primary colours
The **primary colours** are red, yellow, and blue (compare these with the primary light colours). These three colours form a basis from which other colours can be made.

Secondary colours
The colours formed by mixing primary colours are called **secondary colours**. These are orange, green, and violet.

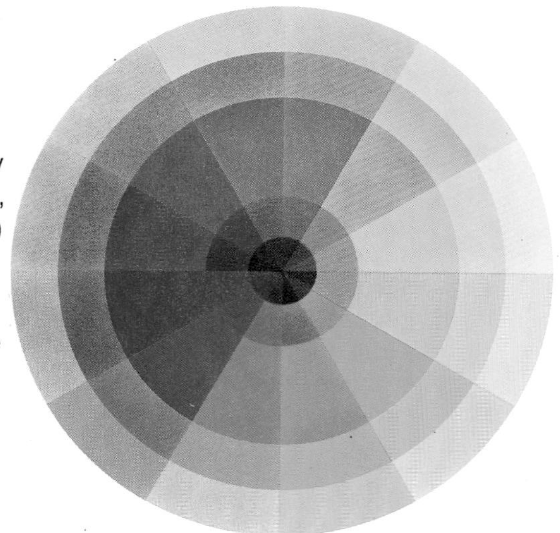

Tertiary colours
These are formed by mixing a primary and a secondary colour. For example, blue (primary) and green (secondary) mix to form blue-green (tertiary).

The colour circle
The colour circle is made up of twelve **hues**. A **tint** of each hue is made by mixing the hue with white. A deeper **shade** is made by mixing a particular hue with black. The word shade is also used to describe the depth or degree of colour.

Each colour's position in the colour circle is important in understanding how colours react with each other.

The colours in the top half of the colour circle are warm and lively. The colours in the lower half are cool, relaxing and give an impression of space.

Complementary colours

Collect sheets of paper or skeins of embroidery cotton in the twelve hues of the colour circle for this activity.

▲ Match each colour:

a with the one diametrically opposite

b with a colour near it on the circle.

What do you notice about the colours in **a**? How does this compare with **b**?

The two colours diametrically opposite each other are called **complementary**. If placed together they **intensify** or **complement** each other. This makes both colours look brighter.

▲ Suggest some colour combinations you would use for things that need to be eye-catching, such as a banner, flag, sports colours on a jacket, an important notice, or the number on a footballer's shirt.

▲ Look at the negative of a colour photograph. Are the colours the same as on the positive? How are they different?

Neutral colours

When two complementary colours are mixed together in equal proportions they cancel each other out, and produce the neutral grey that occurs towards the centre of the colour circle.

▲ Find a piece of neutral grey fabric. Cut it into three small squares. Place one on each of three different coloured fabrics. What do you notice about the neutral grey? Does its colour look the same on each piece of fabric?

When a neutral grey is teamed with a colour, it appears tinged with the colour's complementary partner

▲ Experiment with squares of another colour, and compare that colour's appearance when set against other colours.

By understanding this principle it is possible to assess the effect of putting colours together. Probably the best example of the eye seeing a colour's complementary partner occurs on a sunny day. The orange sun makes the sky appear blue. The brighter the sun, the bluer the sky (and the sea) will appear.

Questions

1 What effect does water have on light rays?

2 What is meant by primary, secondary, and tertiary colours when dealing with fabrics?

3 What is a tint, a shade, a complementary colour?

▲ Using complementary colours, design a logo which would stand out well on your tee-shirt.

Depth and perspective

Sketching

Sometimes artists make a 'frame' with their hands to look at a view. This forms a complete picture. Photographers look at the **composition** of their photograph through a viewfinder to form a complete picture.

▲ Use this technique to look at say the corner of the room, or the window sill. Think of the view as a **line drawing** on a flat piece of paper. Look particularly at the direction of the lines. Notice the angles that they make with other lines, and with the frame of your fingers. Sketch the view.

The sloping lines give **depth** to your sketch.

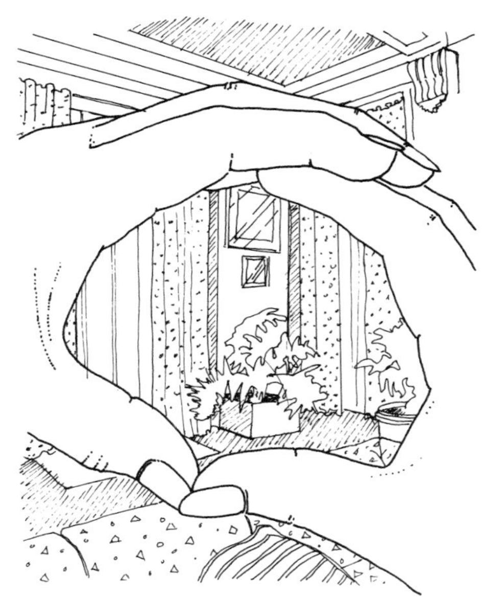

Practise 'view finding' with your hands

Perspective

Distant objects look smaller than the same objects viewed close to. If a flat drawing is to look realistic this fact must be taken into account: the drawing must be in **perspective**. Look at the trees in the opposite sketch.

To ensure that a drawing is in perspective the **vanishing point** is used. Although railway lines are parallel (to allow trains to run on them!), in the sketch they appear to converge. The point at which they meet is known as the vanishing point. If a drawing is in perspective all sloping lines can be extended to meet at this point.

▲ Doodle lines to form a road disappearing into the distance. Complete a sketch by putting something – say a tree – in the foreground, and again in the background (make sure the trees are in proportion in both cases).

▲ Draw a square and make it into a cube by giving it depth. Doodle it: **a** as a sugar lump; **b** as a railway carriage going along the track.
What do you notice about the angle and length of the lines that produce the 'right' shape? The longer the object, the closer the lines move together. The smaller the space between the lines, the more distant it appears.

Now study this picture. Look at the relative sizes of the arches at the front and at the back of the building. The ones at the back look smaller in the drawing although in fact they are the same size. Notice once again the use of sloping lines at the side of the building used to make it look realistic when viewed from the front. Drawing an object to give the same impression of relative positions, sizes, etc, as the actual object does when viewed from a particular point is known as **perspective**.

The impression of nearness, middle distance, or far distance can be achieved by varying the angle of the lines on a drawing. Practise this.

Depth

Look again at the drawing. Which parts are shown in a darker shade? What effect does this have? Depth can be given to a picture by shading. Notice how the darkness gives the impression of going *through* the archway, and looking *inside* the building through the windows. The light shining through the archway also shows the depth of the building. If you half close your eyes the impression of depth becomes clearer. This cuts out detail making the basic shape stand out more.

Dark colours are used for emphasis as well as for depth. The dark colour of the clock face emphasizes the numerals.

All these impressions can be created using textiles.

▲ Make a series of sketches of one object from different angles and distances. Think about depth, perspective, and emphasis. Keep these drawings in your design file.

▲ Take one of these drawings and make a detailed plan of how it could be worked in textiles. Look at the section on transferring designs for guidance, and choose some appropriate techniques like appliqué, quilting, stitching, fabric painting, etc.

Keep the design very simple; it can quite easily be elaborated as you become more proficient.

Combining colours

The choice of colour is the most important decision a designer will make. Before making that decision the effect of combining colours and the impact that each colour will provide, both individually and when combined with others, need to be considered.

Contrast

If two colours appear striking when used together they are said to **contrast** well. Complementary colours contrast well. A good contrast also occurs when light and dark shades of colour are used e.g. pale yellow and dark red. The excellent contrast of black with white is an extreme example of this principle.

Which of these are harmonious and which contrasting colours?

Contrasts can be emphasized by using black or white, since both intensify all other colours. A white border seems to deepen a colour, a black border appears to lighten and brighten one. A black or white line separating colours makes each colour show up more. Decorative features outlined in black or white machine satin-stitching will stand out well.

Harmony

Colours from the same area of the colour circle tone well together, i.e. they produce a pleasing overall effect. These adjacent colours are called **harmonious**. Pastel yellow and deep green, or pale pink and purple, are examples of harmonious colours toning well to produce a gentle and pleasing effect.

▲ Using a shade card or skeins of embroidery thread, experiment with colour to find harmonious and contrasting combinations. Can you *explain* the effects the colours have on each other?

▲ Make a colour circle for your design file.

Colour illusion

Certain colours create particular impressions and seem to possess abstract qualities such as warmth or nearness. Conversely, the complementary partner creates the opposite impression.

The impressions of warmth and coolness, cheerfulness and relaxation, nearness and distance are created by interior designers.

- ▲ Place pieces of different coloured fabrics over a lamp and describe the effect each colour has on the room. Make sure that the light bulb remains cool during the experiment. What colour would you use to decorate a cold room which gets no sunlight? Which colours give the illusion of coolness, distance, and airiness? Why would these be suitable for sunny rooms?

The way we perceive complementary colours is interesting. Stare hard at the red dot on this page for some time. Then either close your eyes completely or look at a white wall. What colour do you see?

The after-image appears green, for the eye always seeks to balance a colour with its complementary partner.

- ▲ Examine the effect of the use of colour in these two pictures. Make a note of how near or far the different features look in each picture. Which colour makes the hills look distant? Which colour makes the sky look distant, and which makes it look close and overcast?

- ▲ Draw a similar simple sketch and make several photocopies of it. Experiment by using different colours in each one and note the effects achieved.

- ▲ Visit a local art-gallery or museum and observe a picture of your choice carefully.

Look at the subject matter. Look at the composition, i.e. where the features of the picture occur in relation to each other. Think about what the artist is trying to express. Discuss how the artist uses colour to convey atmosphere.

Photograph (if you are allowed) or sketch any pictures or objects that make an impression on you in the gallery. Put them in your design file.

The design process

This is the process of designing to meet particular needs i.e. to satisfy a **brief**. The following diagrams show the stages of the design process:

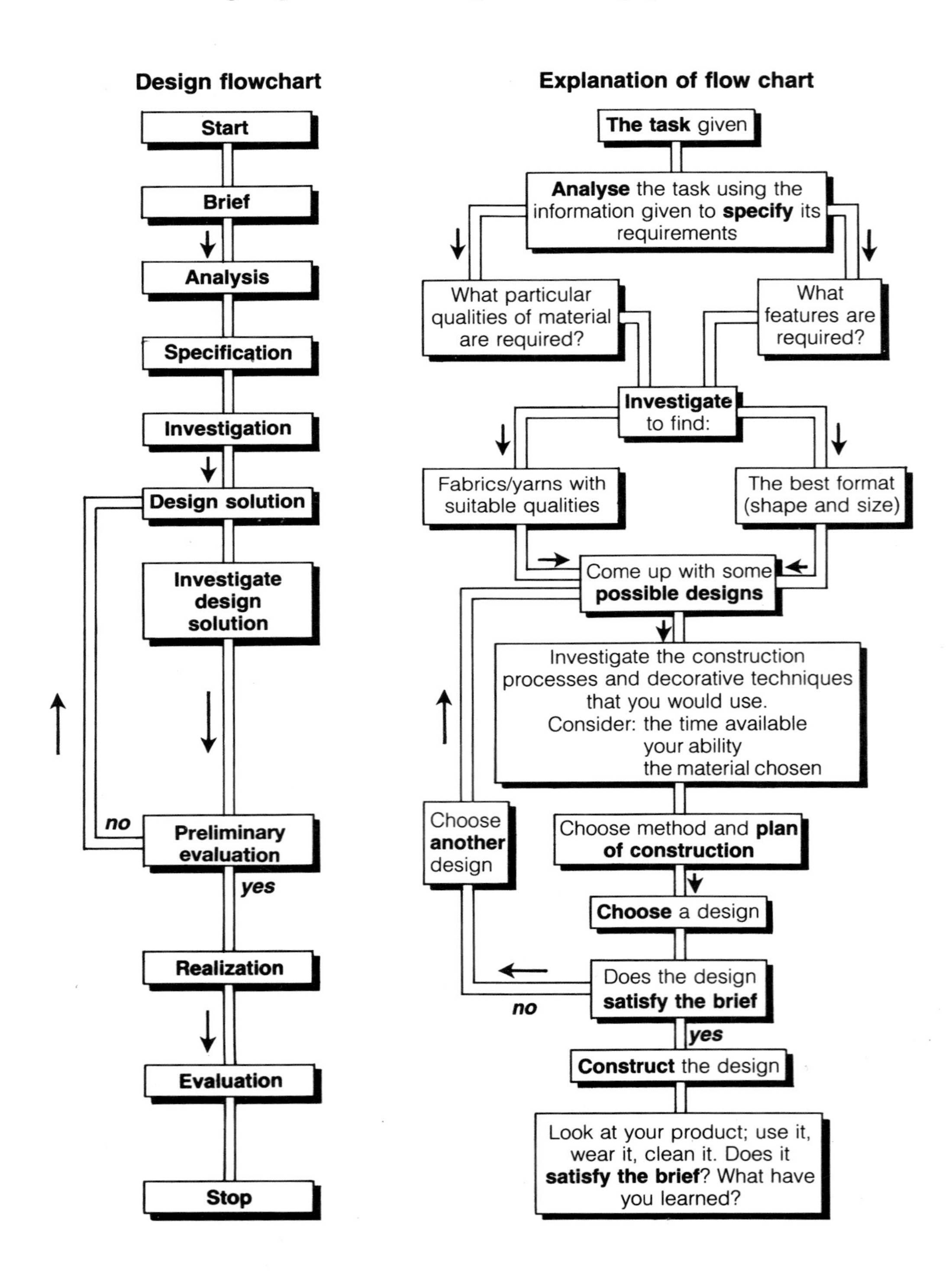

Design and realization

Before starting this section re-read the Introduction.

The brief

The brief is the task that is given to the designer to interpret and realize, e.g. 'design a body warmer' or 'make an all-purpose carrier bag'. The first task in the realization is to analyse the brief and produce a specification which will define the limits within which the design must work. Consider the following example:

Analysis	Specification	Factors affecting design
1 **WHO** will use it?	consider age, ease of handling, interests	aesthetic appeal, size of handles, fastenings
2 **WHY** would they use it?	to carry weight for warmth	fabric qualities such as strength, insulation
3 **WHERE** would it be used? situated? stored?	consider how the item will affect its environment and the effect the environment has on the item	fabric qualities such as water resistance, ease of drying
4 **WHEN** would it be used?	consider wear and tear, how comfortable the item needs to be, whether the item is stored for long periods	reaction to sunlight, detergents, resilience, resistance to damp, of *all* materials used in the design
5 **HOW** would it be used?	consider pressure, strain, and safety	consider safety in using and making

Investigations

The next step in the design process is to find the most suitable materials to fit your specifications. This can be done through investigational work which should include reading, research, and experiments. Fabric qualities and amounts, aesthetic appeal, cost, and availability, should all be considered.

Experimental work
Keep a record of experimental work in your design file as follows:

Aim	what needs to be found out from the experiment
Method	what equipment and techniques were used
Results	what was found out
Conclusion	what can be gathered from the result

Remember to test *all* materials used in the design in the same way e.g. braids, lace, and other decorations.

Question

What human needs and material factors should be taken into account when designing a body warmer?

Design and realization II

Further investigations

Having found by experiment the ideal material required for realizing the brief, the ideal *format* now needs to be investigated.

▲ Make a plan of how you would establish the best format for an item of your choice. Consider what the item has to hold/cover/fit into. Take measurements, and experiment by making the object with paper. Write up your results and conclusions.

The next consideration is the quantity of fabric to be used. Allowances should be made for turnings, growth, and movement.

By conducting experiments and investigations, it is possible to narrow down the choice of materials to those that fit the design specification.

A **design solution** is now in sight. There may be several possible solutions, and each one may be equally good. As the analysis of the brief is a personal one, so too is the solution. It is, however, essential to make sure that the solution meets the needs of the specification, so *keep* checking!

Realization

Once the design solution has been reached a **plan of construction** can begin.

Consider:

a the time available for completion
b the technical ability required
c the chosen materials.

A good realization **fits the specification, is aesthetically pleasing (it looks good!) and is completed in the required time**. This should be worked in fine tapestry as the designer's motto!

Plan of action

The first step is to formulate a **plan of action**. This should consist of a list of processes put in order of construction, and a list of the necessary equipment.

When thinking about processes check back continually to the specification. For example, extra strong seams would be needed for bearing weight or for taking pressure.

When planning the order of construction it is necessary to think about whether, for example, it is easier to put decoration or a zip on to flat fabric before making up.

Consider what equipment would help achieve the best result, e.g. size of needle, type of machine-stitch, iron, etc.

When the plan has been completed, all that remains is to make the item!

Evaluation

The last stage in the design process is the evaluation. Ask yourself the following questions: Does the item realize the brief? If you were making it again would you make any changes? What have you learned? Compare your results with your classmates' realizations.

▲ Using a brief of your choice write a plan of action for its realization. Use the design flowchart (p.22) to help you.

Brief: Design a beach bag

Analysis	Specification		Realization
	What will it have to stand up to?	Qualities needed	Suggested material or fabric
1 **Who will use it?** all the family	constant handling by different age groups	relate style, size and decoration to age and interests of user	bright colours, suitable decoration, or patterned fabric
2 **Why will it be used?** to carry towels, costumes, etc. to the beach, and damp items home	weight and water	light in weight, yet strong, water resistant	strong handles e.g. wooden, or thick smooth cord for shoulder straps
3 **Where will it be used?** on the beach	sun, sand, and sea water	must be washable or wipeable fabric, must not be absorbent, or spoiled by being damp, must dry well	
4 **When will it be used?** often in the summer, stored during winter	bright sunlight and downpours, packing away when not in use	must stand up to strong sunlight, without rotting or fading, water resistant, resilience	heavy duty Polyester, acrylic, PVC, stuffed when stored
5 **How will it be used?** unrestrained use to carry weight	rough handling	suitable size of bag and shoulder straps or handles, tough	suitable size for all ages

Preliminary evaluation

Before realizing a brief, check back to the specifications to see that *each one* is being met. This is called a preliminary evaluation. It makes sure that fabric, shape, and size are all suitable *before* making up.

▲ Evaluate the completed bag shown in the illustration. Is it easy to carry? How does the material chosen react to sunlight and damp storage? What further questions should be asked? Explain the importance of a preliminary evaluation.

Fabric investigations

Grains, stretch, and strength

You will need a variety of fabric scraps of the same size and a pair of scissors for these tests.

Warp and Weft

▲ The **warp** threads run the length of the fabric when it is woven, in the same direction as the selvedge. Choose a piece of woven fabric with a selvedge and pull sharply along the direction of the warp. Does the fabric stretch? Can you hear a snap? The **weft** threads run *across* the warp. Pull sharply along the weft. Do you hear a duller sound? This shows that the weft thread is not so strong and resistant to your pull.

The warp and weft of all woven fabrics can be distinguished in this way. Cut a piece of fabric on the cross and pull it sharply. Does the fabric tear? Along which direction? Why? Can you work out which is the weft (weaker) and warp (stronger) thread of your fabric by doing this experiment?

Stretch and elasticity

The stretch and elasticity of a fabric are important qualities to investigate. The elasticity is a measure of how well a fabric will return to its original shape.

▲ Cut a 30 cm length of yarn, or a 30 cm × 3 cm piece of fabric on the straight grain. Attach a metal nut by tying it on to one end of the yarn, or by stitching it to the end of the fabric. Put graph paper over a board and pin or staple the yarn or fabric on to a horizontal line, so that all the fabrics measure exactly 25 cm from the line to the nut when laid out flat. Stand the board upright. Mark on the paper the distance that each yarn or fabric drops. This shows the stretch or extensibility of the fabric. Leave overnight and mark the amount of stretch of each fabric again the next morning.

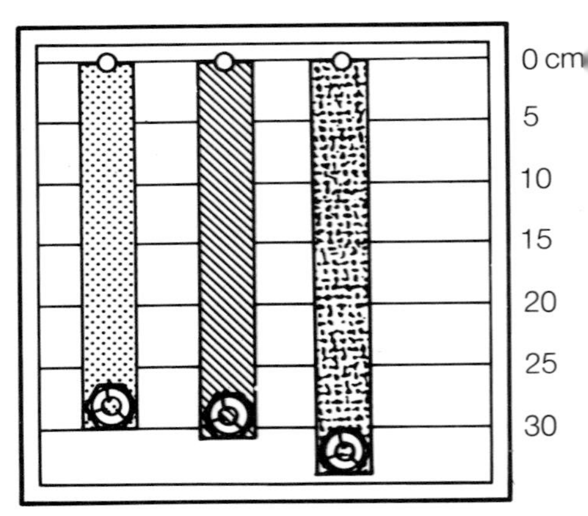

Make a bar chart to show the extensibility of different fabrics.

Next, examine the elasticity of the fabrics. Remove the nut from the fabrics by cutting the stitches or untying the knots. Does the yarn or fabric retract to its original length?

Show the new lengths of the fabric after retracting:

a immediately
b the next day.

Which fabrics are most elastic?

When selecting a fabric for a particular purpose, consider the conditions it will have to tolerate in normal use. You can devise simple experiments to simulate these uses.

Fabric and its environment

▲ Keep squares of wet fabric in saucers of water for a week. Examine them carefully. Then decide which to choose for a beach bag.

▲ Fasten a piece of curtain fabric in a sunny window. Observe any change in colour over a period of time by comparing it with a roll of fabric stored in a cupboard. This will affect your decision as to whether to line curtains.

Fabric testing

Fabrics used together must have similar properties of resilience, water absorption, non-flammability, resistance to sunlight, etc., otherwise they will react differently in use and when washed. Shrinking, puckering, creasing, and fading may occur in certain areas only, but the whole article could be ruined. It could be dangerous if certain items, or even parts of an item, were flammable.

It is a useful exercise to apply tests to all fabrics (especially unidentified ones) and to all decorations such as cording, braid, lace, and other trimmings, before deciding to use them together.

Flammability test
This test:
a gives an indication of the safety of a fabric in use
b helps in identifying fabrics (see *All About Fabrics*).

▲ Always use similar sized pieces when comparing fabrics.

Fabric	**Ignition**	**Description**	**Time elapsed before complete destruction**
A	fast burning	yellow flame	50 s
B	–	self extinguishing	–
C	melts	spits	30 s

Display your findings as a bar chart.

Reaction to water
▲ Collect together uniform pieces of labelled fabrics to be tested. Make a note of the weight of each one. Wash and spin dry all the pieces of fabric together. Weigh each piece of fabric again.

$$\frac{\text{Increase in weight}}{\text{Original weight}} \times 100 = \text{\% water absorbed}$$

Write down the percentage of water absorbed by each fabric and display the results as a bar chart. Leave each piece to dry and compare the drying time.

Evaluate your results.

Colour fastness
▲ Wet the fabric thoroughly. Place it between two layers of white cotton. Press with a hot iron. If the colour is not fast it will run on the white fabric.

Resilience
Crumple the fabric tightly in your hand. Does it spring back to shape or retain creases? A resilient fabric springs back to shape.

Fabric qualities

Fabric	Uses in creative textiles	Yarns, threads, and haberdashery	Texture and warmth
Cotton	*canvas*: rugs, needlepoint *calico*, *drill*, *sailcloth*, *repp*: background fabrics and household items *velveteen*: cushions *lawn*, *cambric*: broderie anglais *organdie*: shadow work *muslin*: backing for Italian quilting	piping cord anchor stranded embroidery and coton à broder anchor machine embroidery thread crochet cotton braids (flammable unless treated) ricrac bias binding cotton lace	firm presses well cool to wear
Linen	*crash*, *holland*: background fabrics *embroidery linen*: counted thread work e.g. drawn thread, cut-out work *table linen* *bed linen*	button twist for strength e.g. in attaching toys' eyes	good conductor of heat cool smooth surface visible threads for embroidery
Hessian	firm background for wall mountings bold embroidery	made from jute or hemp	attractive visible threads strong and coarse
Viscose	substitute for linen or cotton for counted thread work blended with cotton for hardanger	macramé yarn (can stretch)	not warm to wear
Acetate	linings shiny noses on toys	ribbon	may resemble wool or have a silky lustre, often blended with other fibres fairly warm
Tricel	lightweight clothes e.g. blouses quilting lining		drapes well

Questions

1 Why is it important, when buying hessian, to check that it is cut straight by thread?
2 Why should materials used in the same design have similar qualities?
3 Why is viscose sometimes used as a substitute for cotton? What are the disadvantages of doing so?

Fabric	Resilience	Absorbency/ Care label	Ironing	Strength	Flammability
Cotton	poor, can be tebilised (made crease resistant)	good special finishes	iron whilst damp until dry	good, withstands harsh washing affected by mildew, prolonged sunlight, and acids	burns readily unless flame-proofed
Linen	poor	good special finish		as for cotton but resists sunlight	
Hessian	poor	good			
Viscose	poor (cords may stretch)	good, weaker when wet 50		poor, weaker when wet	
Acetate	fairly resilient	not very absorbent 40	it watermarks	moderate strength, affected by long sunlight	burns and/or melts
Tricel	resilient	less absorbent than acetate 'easy care' use anti-stat		stronger than acetate	melts in flame

4 Give two examples of how ribbon can be used as a functional or decorative feature. What factors must be considered when choosing ribbon?

5 Fabrics with a bold thread can be attractively decorated using drawn thread work. Name three materials with a suitable bold weave for this purpose.

Fabric qualities II

Fabric	Uses in creative textiles	Yarns, threads, and haberdashery	Texture and warmth
Nylon	quilting, appliqué blends with other fibres to give strength and better washing qualities *brushed nylon*: smocked nightwear *fine nylon*: shadow work	ropes, cords: macramé soft yarn for knitting etc. braids ribbon lace	can be sheer no natural warmth so brushed for warmth
Polyester	quilting, appliqué *polycotton*: duvet covers quilt wadding duvet or toy stuffing	ropes cords: macramé core spun polyester/ cotton: button thread	wadding filled with trapped air, so light and warm for quilts, duvets, etc.
Acrylic	*acrilan, Courtelle*: warm and knitted dress fabric, suitings *fleecy Courtelle*: dressing gowns *dralon*: curtain fabric *acrylic fur fabric* and *simulated fur*: cushions, jackets, and toys *modacrylic fur:* blended with wool or regenerated fibres	yarns for weaving, knitting, crochet, macramé, and rugs	poor conductor of heat so warm to wear
Wool	coat weight dress weight *felt*: for toys, appliqué *velour cloth*: cushions	yarn of varying plys for weaving, knitting, crochet, macramé, tapestry, embroidery, and rugs	soft warm to wear
Silk	expensive decorative work, ties, cushions, appliqué shadow work fine embroidery particularly Chinese and Japanese	spun silk used for decorative hand or machine work	soft, luxurious, drapes well poor conductor of heat, retains body warmth fineness makes it cool in summer
PVC (Polyvinyl chloride)	can be backed with cotton/nylon aprons bags hats	beware of adding decoration as needle leaves holes use tissue paper under presser foot or use adhesive	outer garments are wind and waterproof; retain air round the body

Fabric	Resilience	Absorbency/ Care label	Ironing	Strength	Flammability
Nylon	good	not absorbent use anti-stat 'easy care'		strong affected by bleach, mineral acid and long sunlight	does not burn melts
Polyester	good	the least absorbent use anti-stat fabric softener to avoid picking up dirt easily 'easy care'	requires little or no ironing	very strong	shrinks away from flame does not burn
Acrylic	good good	not absorbent 'easy care' cold rinse use anti-stat		strong, but tendency to pill when rubbed good	burns then melts modacrylics do not burn
Wool	good	very absorbent	press on WS with damp cloth	stretches or shrinks, handwash and dry carefully, affected by alkali, chlorine, bleach, moths	reluctant to burn
Silk	good	absorbent, but fine, so dries quickly	iron wild silk dry, cultivated silk damp It watermarks	strong in wear do not twist or wring damaged by alkali, bleach, sunlight, perspiration	burns, only slowly
PVC (Polyvinyl chloride)	eventually cracks if left folded	waterproof, wipe to clean		tough damaged by heat cracks if left folded	melts non-flammable

Part II

In Part I the design process and theory of realizing a brief was discussed. Part II looks at the techniques needed to put that theory into practice.

Transferring designs

The first technique required is transferring your chosen design to your chosen material.

Using graph paper

One way you can transfer your design is to use graph paper. Look at the method below.

Method

Here is a drawing marked out on graph paper. It is part of the design featured on a sweater.

1 When knitting, the squares on the graph represent stitches, change colour wool when you reach a cross (p.61).
2 A design on appropriate sized graph paper may be placed behind a loom to act as a guide when picture weaving (p.53).
3 The squares can represent knots in the same way when designing a rug. But rug backing has large thread lines anyway. It is quite easy to draw the design full size on it, using the lines just like graph paper. Your drawing would be covered by the knots, and would not show when the rug is complete.

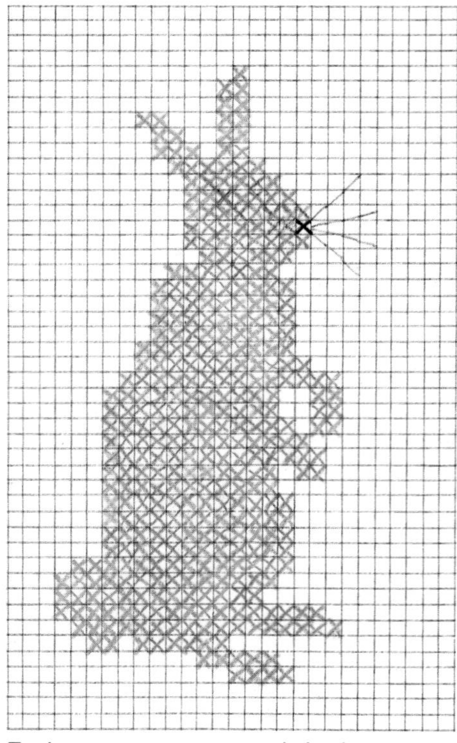

Each cross represents a stitch when knitting or embroidering

Marking fabric

To transfer a design it is often necessary to mark the fabric. But some marks do not wash out of material. Also there are some fabrics (and articles) that we may not want to wash. Experiment with the numerous fabric markers available.

Building up designs

Modify your design to suit the area or shape to fill, your ability, the time available, and your materials.

Here is an example of building up a design. This design also shows how the impressions of depth and perspective can be created in textile work. It is meant as a guide only but some of the ideas will be useful to you when transferring and building up your own designs. Before beginning construction make a plan of work.

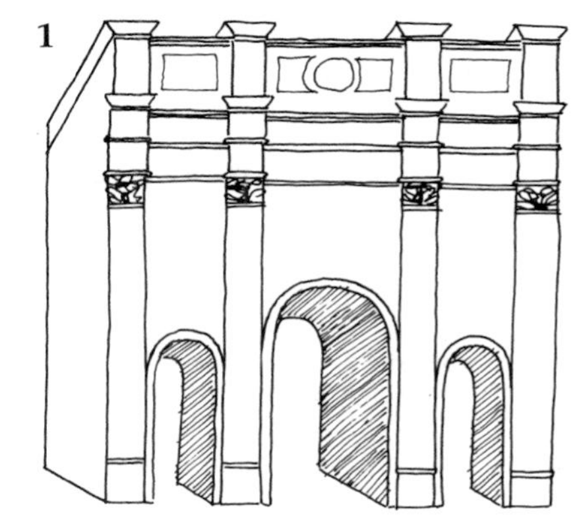
1

Plan of work

1 Select materials and colour scheme. Trace the outline of the drawing on to graph paper. Now draw it up to size on larger squared paper and make a full-size tracing from it. Cut inner archway sections to use for patterns.

2 Lay some fine white fabric across the lower section of backing fabric and wadding. Lay some fine black fabric over the white fabric. Place your tracing on top, and mark the position of inner archways with fabric pencil or tailor's chalk. Remove the tracing. Matching marks carefully, tack inner archway patterns on to the fabric. Machine satin stitch around the edges and remove patterns. Cut away the black fabric beneath to reveal the white inner section.

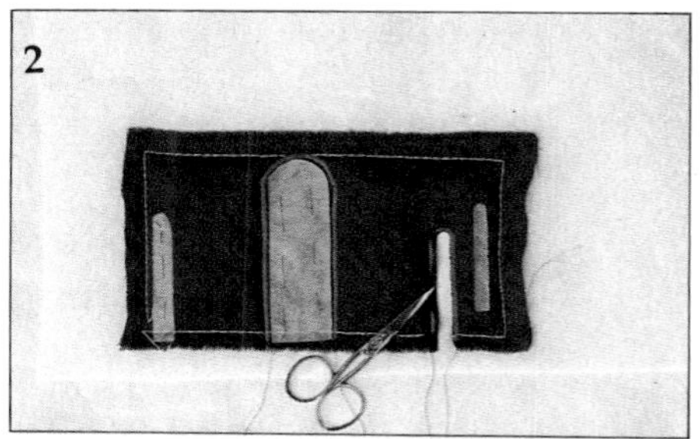
2

3 Tack the rest of the tracing to the right side of some blue fabric. Machine decorative lines as shown. Cut columns in two layers of polyester wadding. Tack to the wrong side of blue fabric. Lay the blue fabric over the base and tack.

3

4 Machine up sides of columns with a straight stitch. Machine around archway with satin stitch. Machine 0.5 cm away with straight stitch. Starting at the bottom draw piping cord through, and then snip it off.

5 Machine lines across base to complete your design. If you do not wish to use tracing paper, fabric marker will be a good substitute.

▲ Draw a simple realistic design and make a plan of work showing how you would construct it. Pay particular attention to the ideas of depth and perspective.

4

Construction techniques

This section looks at the construction techniques that are used in all aspects of creative textiles, and how they may be used to realize briefs.

Making patterns

The first step is to decide on the best shape and size of the item by **analysis** and **specification**.

Sketch the item from different angles. Decide on how many pieces of fabric will be required and what each should measure. Remember to allow for turnings and seam allowances. Draw each piece on paper and cut out.

It is often useful to make a paper mock-up of the item. By trial and error you will get it right! Label each piece clearly and use it as a pattern and to estimate the quantity of fabric required.

Estimating quantity

Lay the pattern pieces on a rectangular table as close together as possible.

a The selvedge of the (imaginary) fabric should run from the top to the bottom of each piece.

b Keep within the width that fabric is sold in (or half the width if it is folded).

Measure the length of the fabric required.

Make construction easy for yourself

1. Clearly label each pattern piece.
2. After cutting out, mark all design and construction points clearly with fabric marker, tailor's chalk, or tailor's tacks.
3. Use the iron to keep fabric smooth and flat throughout construction. It is useful to press seams as you go along and *not just* after completion.
4. Work is always easier to handle when flat. Positioning, pinning, and machining are firmer and more accurate when done directly over a flat surface, where nothing can get caught beneath.
5. Plan your order of work.

Look at these examples of realized briefs and notice the construction techniques used in each case.

Beach bag in nylon backed PVC

NB When using PVC, simulated suede, or leather, tape seams to avoid pinholes, or use clips. A teflon coated foot prevents sticking.

Order of work

1. Fold braid over top edges.
2. Attach zip and decorate bag with braid.
3. Stamp eyelets.
4. Make darts (optional).
5. Join side seams using piping.
6. Turn to right side. Pull cord through and knot firmly.

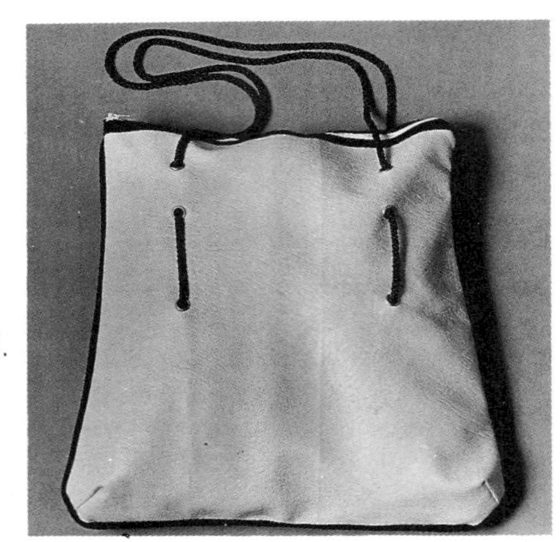

Techniques

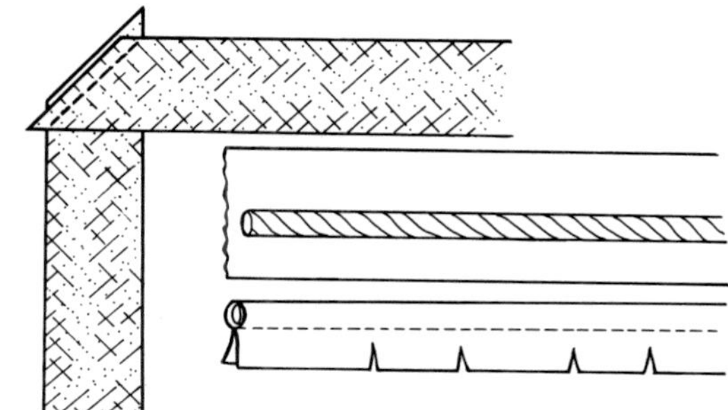

Crossway or bias strips (bias binding) will stretch around the curves of your piped bag. Use crossway strips to cover piping cord. Use a zipper foot to machine close to the cord. Clip turnings when used on a curve.

A quilted tissue box cover

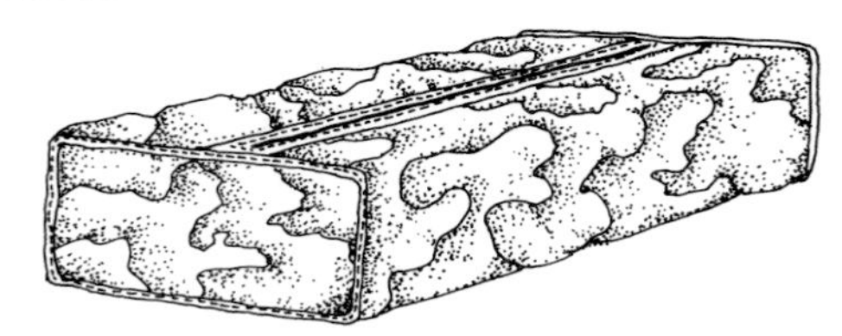

Here are details for the construction of a box cover.

What fabrics would be suitable? In what widths are these usually available? Can you work out the quantity required? Make a shopping list of all the materials needed to make the cover.

1. Cut out and quilt the fabric as desired (p.42).
2. Tack the shorter sides of the large piece right sides together 1.5 cm from the edge.
3. Machine for 4 cms at each end of the seam. Leave the tacking stitches in to hold the folded edges together until the zip is completed. Press open.
4. Put a closed zip in position beneath the seam. Tack. Machine the zip into position on right side with cover turned inside out to keep other fabric *above* the machine needle.
5. Pin and tack end panels in position with wrong sides together, and raw edges on right side.
6. Tack bias binding evenly over raw edges.
7. Machine through all thicknesses using three step zig-zag. Remove tacks.

▲ Design a container to be used for stamps.

Decide on the size, and work out how to make the mock-up in cardboard. Make a list of the items you would need to construct and the materials required to cover the box. Suggest suitable materials for the outside, and the lining, giving reasons for your choice. On graph paper draw and colour the design for the lid.

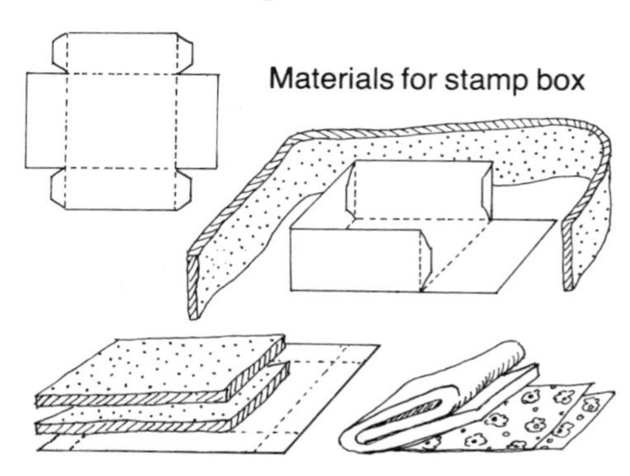

Materials for stamp box

Fabric painting

One of the easiest techniques in creative textile work is fabric painting. It's fun and it gives quick results.

Preparation

Wash and dry the chosen fabric first so that the paint is taken up by the fabric. (Starch and other fabric treatments hamper the absorption of colour by the fabric.)

Spread the fabric (single thickness) over a hard surface. Anchor it securely to prevent slipping by pinning or stapling it to card, or by bulldog-clipping it over a piece of formica.

Paints

You can buy fabric paint in small pots and apply it directly to the fabric with a small soft brush. The strokes should be applied along the grain for even colour, this is particularly important on a knitted fabric such as is used for tee-shirts.

Watering the paint slightly produces a paler shade. Fabric paints, like ordinary ones, can be mixed to produce new colours. The shade of these can be varied by using more or less of each colour.

If you want to paint on dark fabric apply a coat of white paint to it first. This ensures that the actual applied colour appears on the fabric and not a darkened version of it.

Spray diffuser

Applying paint with a spray diffuser produces a most attractive muted effect. You can buy a diffuser from an art or craft shop. Cut-out shapes in sticky paper attached to fabric before spraying leave the shape outlined on the fabric when peeled off. The design can then be emphasized with machine stitching, quilting, fabric crayon, or painting. Alternatively a spray diffuser can be used to give colour to a background fabric e.g. for a collage.

Take a deep breath!

Crayons

Non-toxic dye sticks can also be bought at an art or craft shop. These should also be applied in one direction only to give an even colour. Dye sticks can be sharpened and used like crayons to give lines or fine edges to a design.

When you repeat a design take care to wipe the formica before moving the fabric along, to avoid smudging it.

Potato cut-outs and card stencils are techniques for printing repeat designs on to fabric

Setting

Heat *sets* the colour on fabric. Mistakes can be removed by washing *before* setting. When the design is finished, allow the fabric to dry completely. Then iron the painting between two layers of cotton cloth or paper with a very hot iron for about two minutes to set the paint (the iron must be kept moving). After setting the colour is *fast* when washed.

Transfers

A design coloured on paper with dye or fabric paint can be used as a transfer, and ironed face down on to a fabric before it dries. It will then set on the fabric with the heat of the iron.

Synthetics do not stand up to the high temperatures required to set dye into fabric but protection with a cotton cloth solves this problem. It is necessary to check that the colours to be used are suitable for synthetics before attempting to use them on these fabrics.

The transferred design forms a basis for further decoration with, say, embroidery.

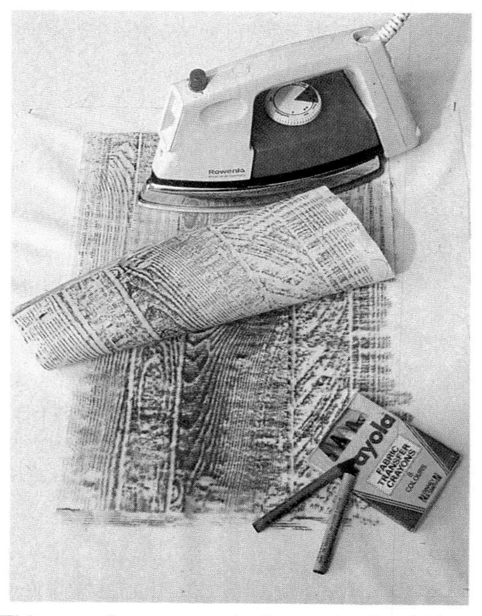

This transfer was made from a bark rubbing

▲ Design a duvet cover and make it up with fabric paint. Think of the different methods you can use to emphasize and create patterns. Use as many as you can. Design wall paper and curtains to match the duvet. You might choose a repeat design or a contrasting one.

▲ Invent a striking flag and make it using fabric paint.

Questions

1. Why is it important to wash fabric before painting?
2. Describe three ways in which paint or dye can be applied to fabric.
3. How could you make a stencil or template for a repeat design?
4. How could you transfer a picture on to fabric?
5. What makes painting *fast* on fabric?

Smocking

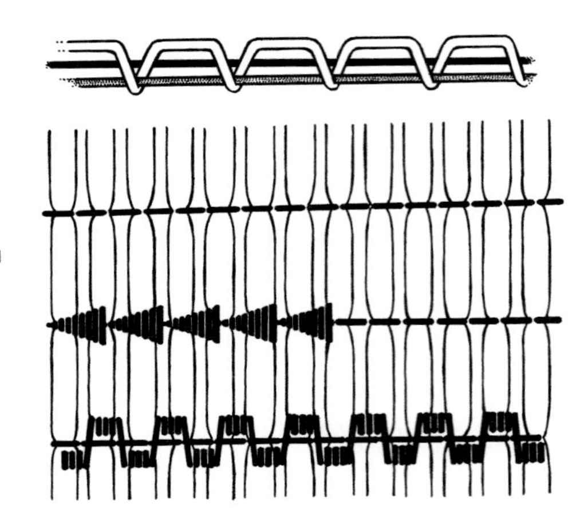

Quick smocking

Method

1 Make lines of machine gathering 1 cm apart. Use a large stitch and loosen the top tension.
2 Gather by pulling the bottom thread. Knot the ends and sew them in for security and neatness.
3 Now begin the smocking, there are a few different ways of doing so:
   a use a decorative machine stitch over the gathered lines
   b use small ric-rac to form diamond shapes between the gathered lines

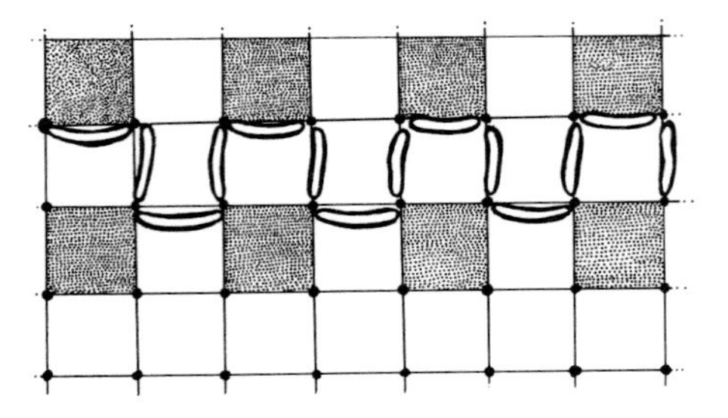

Hand smocking

Look in *All About Fabrics* (p.167) for the technique of smocking and try it out on gingham.

Smocked cushions

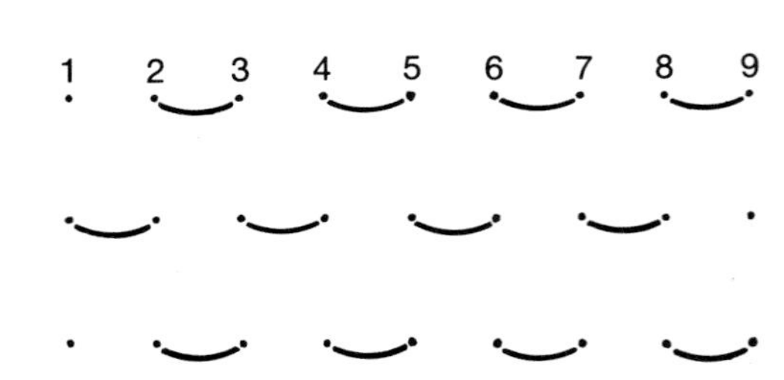

The way in which the fabric falls on the reverse side of a smocked area is made use of in soft furnishing. Smocked cushions in velvet, velour, or velveteen are easy to make. Use a strong button thread.

Method

The smocking is done on the *wrong side* of the material by hand.

1 Mark smocking dots on the wrong side as shown. Stitch with button thread from left to right.
2 Draw dots 3 and 2 together and secure with a small stitch. Do the same to dots 5 and 4.
3 Continue working as shown in the diagram. Work the next line by drawing dots 2 and 1 together. The distance between lines is limited by the size of fold that is required.

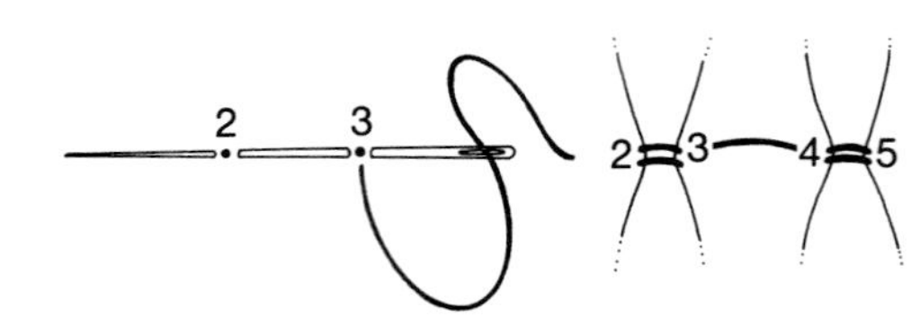

The folds of fabric that form on the right side can be used to make a bolster, a round cushion, or a pouffe.

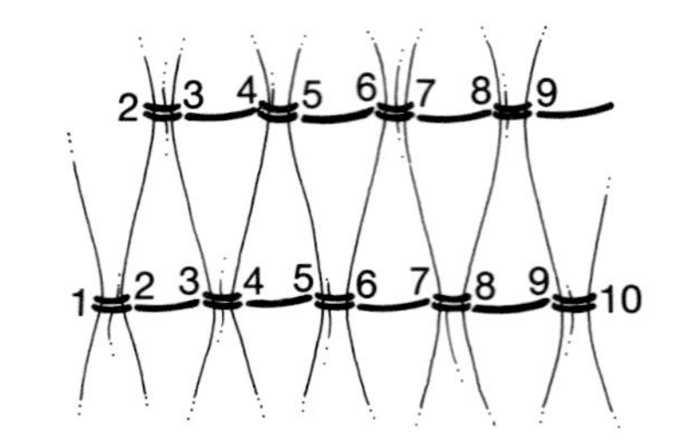

▲ **Design and make a pouffe cover using approximately 1.5 m of furnishing fabric.**

Smocking would be a suitable technique to use for realizing this brief.

Method

1 Design the pouffe and make decisions on size, shape, and material. Synthetics, cottons, velveteen, and velour are suitable materials but the final choice of fabric will depend on how the pouffe is to be used.
2 Make a scale drawing of the pouffe.

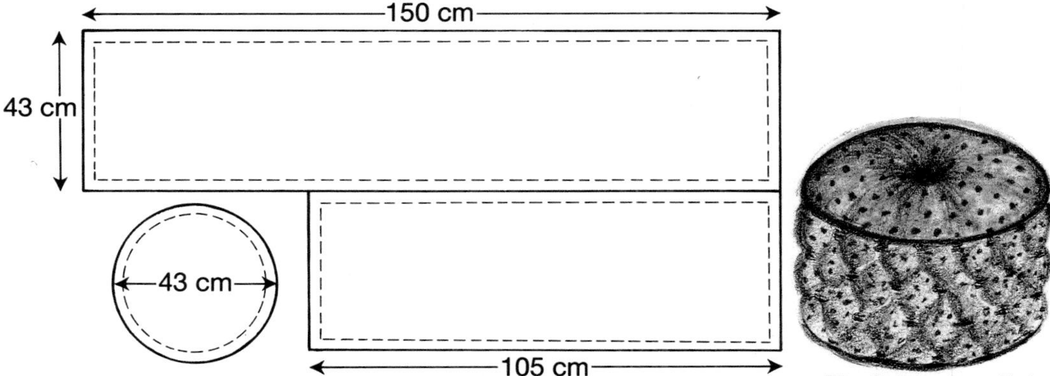

The finished pouffe!

3 Estimate the amount of fabric required.
Measure the diameter of the pouffe (or work it out from the scale drawing). Knowing the diameter of the pouffe the circumference can be calculated.

Circumference = diameter × π $\pi = 3.14$

With a diameter of 40 cm the circumference would be 126 cm. You will need the fabric to be twice that length to allow for smocking. (Allow 1.5 cm around each piece.)

You can lay out the material as shown in the diagram, assuming the diameter and depth of the pouffe are both 40 cm.

Calculate the amount of fabric required in the width in which it can be bought.

4 Cut out the fabric.
5 Join the side pieces together to make a strip of fabric 255 cm long. Mark dots 3 cm apart along the wrong side of the fabric. Decide on the width between smocking rows and mark this as well.
6 Smock two lines along until the length of the drawn up fabric equals the length of the proposed circumference. Cut off the extra fabric leaving enough for the seam and to link the smocking evenly. Complete the smocking.
7 Pin the top line of the smocking to the cut out circle (right-sides together). Tack and sew.
8 Complete base of cover, there are two ways:
 a simple removable cover:
 Bind bottom edge attaching tying tapes at eight places. Tie underneath pouffe. Use 2.5 m of tape and some bias binding.
 b sewn on cover:
 Cut out a 43 cm circle of strong or heavy duty fabric. Machine stitch the base to the sides, right sides together, one third of the way round. Press remainder of turnings on base to wrong sides. Place cover over pouffe and pin and oversew neatly.

Working with dye

Tie-and-dyeing

The art in tie-and-dyeing is to prevent parts of the fabric absorbing the dye. You can knot it, twist it, gather it, or bind it with string, so that the dye is taken up to varying degrees giving different patterned effects.

Method

1 Prepare your garment or fabric completely at random, or form a regular pattern carefully.

Experiment by inventing your own knots

2 Select a dye suitable for the fabric, and follow the maker's instructions in mixing and using it.
3 Wash the fabric and leave it wet. It will absorb the dye better.
4 Immerse the whole fabric, or just the knots, in the dye. Allow to soak for the required time.
5 Rinse thoroughly until the colour has stopped coming out. Undo the knots or twists and rinse again.
6 Test for colour fastness by ironing a small piece until dry between two layers of white cotton fabric. There should be no dye on the cotton.
7 Iron the whole thing whilst damp.

You can repeat the operation using different colours to achieve a variety of effects. A tied and dyed fabric provides a good starting material for embroidery or appliqué.

Batik

▲ Wash a piece of cotton cloth to remove any finish or dressing. Cut into two parts. Brush one piece with melted wax. Notice the effect on the appearance of the fabric. Put a little water on the surface of both pieces. Is the water absorbed? Note the result. What conclusion do you draw?

Fabric may be painted with wax to make it water repellent. This is the basis of the ancient art of **batik**, or painting in wax, still practised in Indonesia. Waxed fabric resists water and cannot take up dye.

▲ Stretch out a piece of washed cotton fabric. Paint shapes in wax with a brush. Allow to set. Immerse it in a cold-water dye according to the dye makers instructions. Rinse, dry carefully, and remove wax (4).

Traditionally, the pattern used in batik involves dots and lines because it is done with a **tjanting tool** – a small copper vessel with a lid and a fine spout. Experts can use a vessel with two spouts to trail very beautiful and intricate designs on to fabric. The colours white, blue, and brownish-black feature prominently in ethnic batik, though any cold water dyes can be used.

Designs are often drawn from nature incorporating birds, plants, etc.

▲ To practise batik you will need:

Wax – a good mixture would be 75% paraffin wax and 25% beeswax
a tin
a bristle brush to wax larger areas
a frame on which to stand the fabric
cold water dyes (e.g. blue and yellow)
an iron
a saucepan
a tjanting tool
panel pins
newspaper

Method

Choose white cotton fabric without a special finish. Wash it to remove any dressing. Make a design featuring dots and lines. A bristle brush can be used for larger areas to be waxed. Decide which areas are to be white, blue, or green.

1 Stretch out the fabric on a frame and pin firmly.
Place 75% paraffin wax and 25% beeswax in little pieces in a tin. Place the tin in a pan of warm water. Heat gently to melt the wax. Keep the water at simmering point. When the wax is melted, partly fill the tjanting tool. Use the lid or a saucer to prevent any unwanted drips falling on the fabric. Trail wax on to the areas to be left white. Brush any larger areas to be waxed. Allow the wax to set on the fabric.

2 Prepare a blue cold water dye according to the dye makers instructions. For example use 1 tin Dylon Cold, 1 sachet cold fix, and 120 g salt for each 100–150 g dry weight of fabric. Immerse the prepared fabric in the blue dye for the appropriate time, say 1 hour. Remove and rinse the fabric in cold water, till it runs clear. Allow it to dry, away from the heat.

3 Wax the parts to be left blue.
Immerse the prepared fabric in cold-water yellow dye. The wax resists the dye, and only the unwaxed blue part turns green. Rinse and dry.

4 Remove the wax by ironing the fabric between sheets of newspaper. The warmth of the iron melts the wax into the paper. If the fabric is still stiffened by wax, a little white spirit can be used carefully to remove it. Finally wash the fabric normally in warm water. Rinse well and iron. Batik work can be used as a basis for building up more complicated designs.

▲ Now make your own patterns. Limit yourself to two or three colours at first. Bold patterns in only two colours can be very effective.

Quilting

Quilting is a very useful technique which is both decorative and warm. The polyester wadding placed between two layers of fabric gives warmth and thickness.

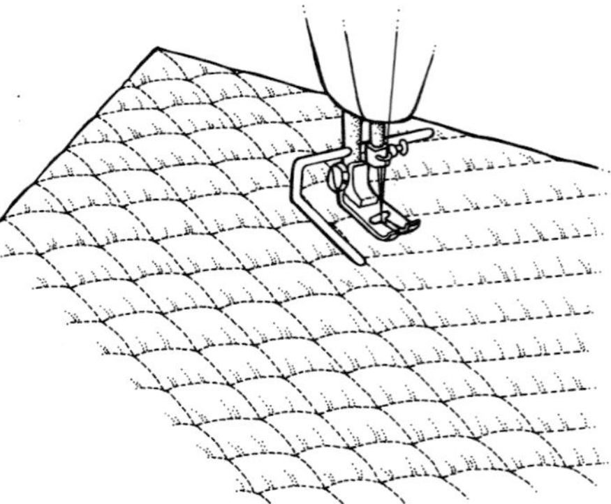

Block quilting

Method

1. Spread the fabric and wadding on a flat surface as shown.
2. Use long pins to pin the three layers together. Start in the centre and work outwards, pinning then tacking at about 15 cm intervals.
3. Mark the centre line of the 'sandwich' with tacking stitches to prevent the fabric slipping.
4. Prepare the machine for quilting. Choose a suitable thread and a longer stitch than you would normally allow for the fabric. Use a quilting foot; this has short upturned toes to allow the thick wadding to flow easily beneath the foot. The crossbar attached to the quilting foot can be adjusted to run along the previous line of stitching. Even, parallel lines are assured by using this as a guide.
5. Begin quilting along the centre line and start *each* line from the same end.

   Block quilting may be done along the grain of the fabric to form squares, or diagonally to form diamonds. Other effects can be produced by using wavy lines, free quilting (simply make patterns of machine stitching over the three thicknesses), or by using different machine stitches e.g. three step zig-zag.

▲ Quilt a motif onto a waistcoat.
Stamp or draw the outline onto the backing fabric. Then, on the wrong side, machine along the outline very carefully.

To make the motif stand out more clearly it may be padded separately.

1. Place the pieces of wadding between the fabrics where motifs are to be and tack in position.
2. Stitch around the motif.
3. Carefully trim the wadding outside the stitching line with embroidery scissors.

To finish the edges of block quilting

A quilted section of an article is joined to the other parts by seams. The excess padding can be trimmed away from turnings with sharp scissors before the seam is neatened.

Block quilted items may be bound with matching or contrasting crossway fabric. This method is especially suitable for curves such as armholes and necklines. For items with straight sides, or where quilting does not come right to the edge, single turnings should be made on both the main and backing or lining fabric. Machine on the edge, or slip stitch by hand, to secure.

Italian quilting

Italian quilting has a raised outline which is padded with yarn *after* stitching, and adds texture to a design.

Method

1 Draw the design on to an interlining fabric such as lightweight muslin or vilene.
2 Place the lining wrong sides together with the main fabric (with no padding between) and tack together.
3 Machine the designed outline with two parallel lines of stitching so that padding yarn can be threaded through. Make sure that the lines do not cross each other.
4 Using **padding yarn** and a tapestry needle draw the yarn through between the lines of stitching. Clip the interfacing at corners in order to pull the needle and yarn through before re-inserting it.
5 A further layer of fabric should be used to line Italian quilting if the wrong side is to be visible.

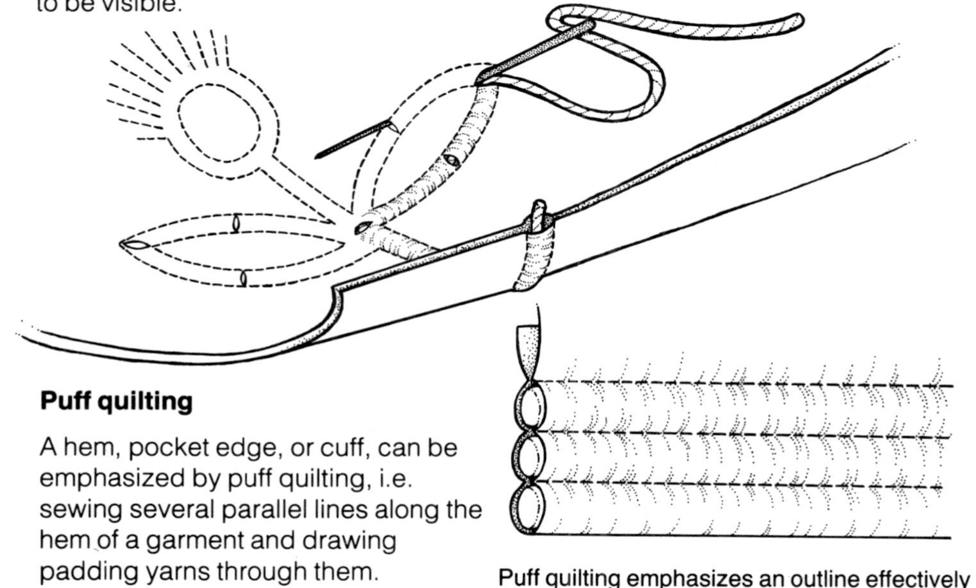

Puff quilting

A hem, pocket edge, or cuff, can be emphasized by puff quilting, i.e. sewing several parallel lines along the hem of a garment and drawing padding yarns through them.

Puff quilting emphasizes an outline effectively

Questions

1 Why is interlining used in Italian quilting? Why should this type of quilting be lined too.

2 List the qualities required in materials for making a sponge or toilet bag. Sketch a simple design. Looking at the chart on p.28–30, select a suitable combination of fabrics. Are there any that you might avoid? Why?

3 Sketch three matching containers in quilted cotton fabric which could be used on a dressing table or for travelling.

▲ Design a quilted toilet, cosmetic, or beach bag, and line it with PVC.

▲ Quilt a cushion cover using a design of your choice. Say where you would use the finished cushion.

▲ Design and make a gift box, a sports bag, or a box file to hold telephone numbers using free quilting.

Appliqué

Appliqué is the application of one piece of fabric to another. The fabric shape to be appliquéd should be cut so that its warp and weft threads match the background material when it is sewn in place.

Methods of appliqué

1 *By hand*
Herringbone stitch can be used to appliqué fabrics which fray. Other fabrics can be applied by embroidery or tiny hem stiches with a turned or unturned edge.

2 *By machine*
Satin stitch width 2 or 4 and length 0.3 can be used to machine around the shapes in matching or contrasting cotton. The stitching line should be trimmed close with sharp scissors.

Zig-zag stitch secures appliqué firmly and prevents fraying. Three step zig zag is especially suitable for towelling where the stitches are invisible.

Edge stitch may also be used to appliqué fabrics after turning. The turnings should be pressed to the wrong side and the corners clipped and mitred. Then the fabric may be pinned, tacked, and edge-stitched into position. This method is suitable for patches and pockets.

Shirring stitch is used for applying stretchy fabric.

Appliqué can be used to create both striking and peaceful effects

3 *Fusing*
▲ You need some bondaweb – a soft adhesive attached to special paper – for this activity:

- **a** draw the shape on the paper and cut it out
- **b** iron it on to the fabric, leave to cool
- **c** peel off the paper
- **d** place the pre-cut fabric shape on the adhesive
- **e** cover with a damp cloth and press with a hot iron until dry
- **f** cool well before testing the adhesive strength
- **g** embroider over the appliqué if necessary,

4 *Using vilene*
Iron-on interfacing may be used to back a fabric shape before appliqué. This gives extra firmness to the appliquéd shape.

If a nursery character, for example, is to be applied on to a baby's stretch suit, vilene should be used to back this stretchy fabric before cutting out the shape. This gives extra firmness to the *area* where the motif is to be placed. Excess vilene may be peeled off when the work is completed.

Special effects with appliqué

Padded appliqué
Place a layer of wadding beneath the fabric shape to be appliquéd. Appliqué by hand or machine. This makes the fabric shape stand out more and adds textural interest to your whole design.

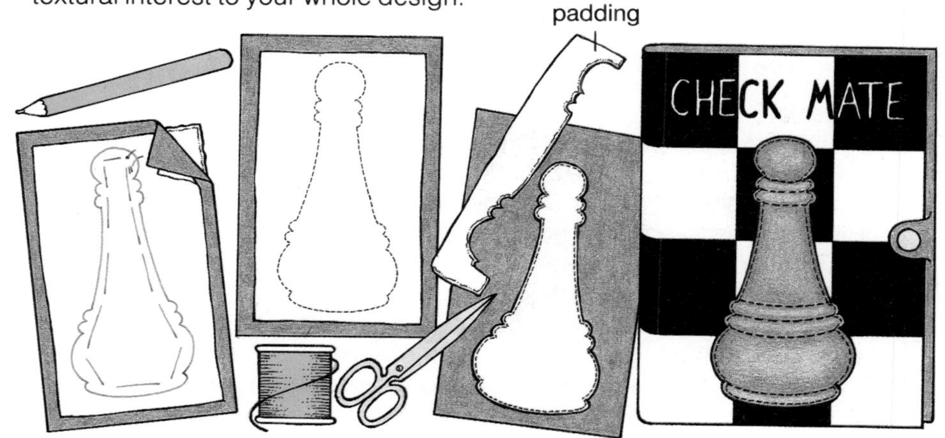

Step-by-step padded appliqué

Shadow work
A design in lightweight coloured fabric is appliquéd on to the *wrong side* of a see-through material such as organza or net. It is used for effects of water, mist, butterflies, or to create a dream-like impression.

By hand, the shapes are applied with herring-bone stitch in sewing silk on the wrong side. The outline is emphasized by the stitching which appears clearly on the right side as two parallel rows of running stitch. Alternatively, machine stitching may be used to emphasize the mute colour of the fabric shape with a bold outline on the right side.

▲ Cut out strips of as many different types of fabric as you can find. Experiment with the techniques outlined on this page to find the best method for each material.

Questions

1 Why is herring-bone stitch used to appliqué coarse cotton?
2 Describe three methods of appliqué which cause strikingly different effects.
3 What do you understand by the term appliqué? Describe how you would use it when designing a wall hanging.
4 Traditionally, appliqué stitches are made as invisible as possible. Why do you think this is so?

Macramé

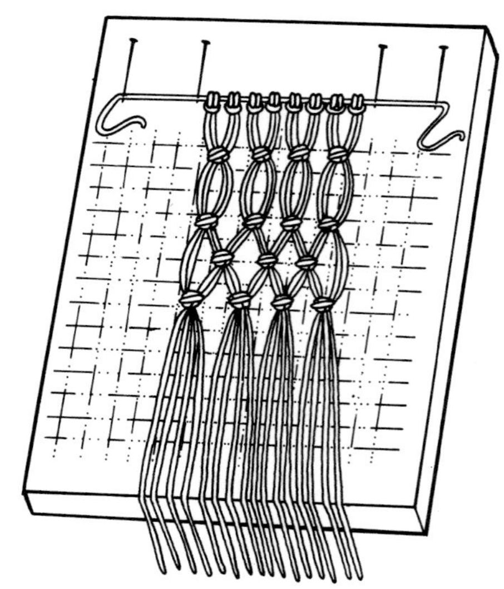
The knots are held in position

Macramé uses knots to make attractive articles to wear and for the home. Parcel string (natural, or softened and coloured by cold-water dyeing), synthetic cord, rug wool, jute, in fact virtually any thread, can be used. The texture, appearance, and size of the finished item will vary accordingly. Stretchy yarns should be avoided.

If you are a beginner choose jute, a light serviceable cord which makes attractive household items.

Method

All you need is a piece of cork board, some string and some T pins. **The macramé board** is made of cork or fibre. It is usually about 30 cm × 40 cm and marked in squares so that the work stays even. You can make your own. Rule it into squares to act as a guide, or stick 1 cm or 2 cm squared paper on to it.

T pins are sold in packets at craft shops. Use them to anchor the cord, and to hold the knots as you work.

Lay a spreader or holding cord across the top of the board. Secure it with T pins. This is the string which holds the working cords.

Fold each working cord in half, and secure with a lark's head (see next page) to produce hanging ends as shown in the diagram.

Practise the knots, forming your own design as you go along. For example, square knots 2 or 3 cm apart make a lampshade or bottle cover grow quickly.

A macramé plant-pot holder

Set eight lark's heads on to a wooden or metal ring. Work a few knots to make a firm start. This is the hanger. Pin it to the centre of an upturned bowl. Anchor to a coat hook and spread the cords so that they hang evenly down the sides of the bowl. Using the illustrated knots, work your own design. (The space between the knots must be large enough, at some point, to fit the plant pot through.) When the net is long enough, the threads can be drawn together at the ends to form a tassel. Alternatively a circular wooden board may be used. Each cord should be drawn through a hole in the base and secured with overhand knots.

Some knots

Lark's head
Fold the cord in half.
Lay it over the holding cord at right angles to it.
Draw the ends through.

A **square knot** uses four cords or multiples of four. It is a reef knot worked around the two inner cords. Also known as flat, Solomon's macramé, or sailor's knot.

Half hitch worked as blanket stitch.

Clove hitch. Two half hitches. Each cord can be clove hitched around a horizontal or diagonal leader, the cord which leads the direction of knotting.

A **sinnet** is a series of knots worked one beneath the other.

Questions

1. What types of yarn can be used for macramé? Which are unsuitable?
2. What is a sinnet and a holding cord?
3. Suggest three ways of using end cords, say where you might use each method.

Ways with embroidery

Embroidery is the decoration of fabric using thread. Striking effects can be created very simply by careful choice of colour, threads, and fabrics. More detailed embroidery requires patience and care.

Tools

You will need a **crewel needle** with a long eye, through which embroidery thread can easily pass. A pair of embroidery scissors with small sharp blades will be useful, as will an **embroidery ring** (the fabric is fitted between the inner and outer ring to keep it flat and to prevent the stitches being pulled too tightly).

Materials

A firm, strong, and even-weave fabric such as hessian is a useful background material for beginners. To ensure that your background material *stays* in the background avoid bold prints or brightly woven fabrics.

Threads
Collect together as many different types of thread as you can. Include cotton, silk, wool, synthetic, metallic, and even plastic threads. Keep an example of each in your design file, you could arrange them in colours.

Choose a thread to match the background fabric in type and weight.

The stitches

Below is a selection of simple embroidery stitches.

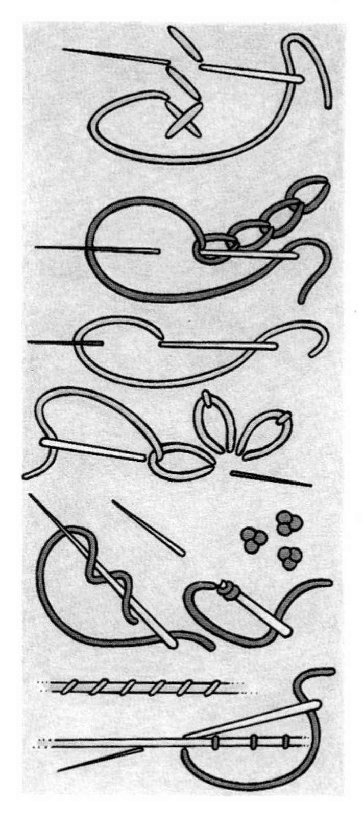

Cross stitch
A very simple stitch which, when used imaginatively, gives impressive effects.

Chain stitch
This is used for lines and can be worked in a variety of threads. Hold the work in the left hand and point the needle towards yourself.

Lazy daisy
This is a large single chain stitch held down by a small tail. It is often used for flower petals.

French knots
Used as a filling stitch to give colour or texture to an area, e.g. the centre of flowers, or spots of an animal.

Twist the thread around the needle. Point it into the fabric in almost the same spot as it came out. Bring the needle out on the right side ready for the next stitch.

Couching
A slanting (occasionally straight) stitch used to hold thick threads laid on a surface. A matching finer thread is usually used.

▲ Make an experimental wall panel. Obtain a remnant of curtain material and enhance the pattern with as many different stitches as you can. (Look in the many available embroidery books for new stitches.) It is a good idea to work the same stitch in patches using different threads for comparison.

Which stitches make good 'fillers'? Which catch the eye? Update your experimental panel as you learn new stitches.

Machine embroidery

Experiment with your machine to see what effects you can create (e.g. free machining). Read the instruction book thoroughly, it can be a mine of useful information.

Some machines are able to make intricate embroidery patterns. If you have access to one, read the instructions and experiment on your panel. These stitches are particularly effective on borders.

▲ Design and make your own coat of arms using free machining.

Patchwork

Patchwork involves joining pieces of material together. Interesting shapes and patterns can be made using squares, diamonds, triangles, pentagons, etc., as well as the more traditional hexagons.

Choice of colours

Look back at the section on colour (p.20).

Which colour combinations would make patchwork striking? Could the base fabric of the cushion, curtain, or hat add to that effect? Which colours would give a more restful effect?

The colour combination is as important as the patchwork design itself. Before choosing colours consider the effect you want the article to achieve in its surroundings.

Traditional hand patchwork

This method is used for all shapes of patches.

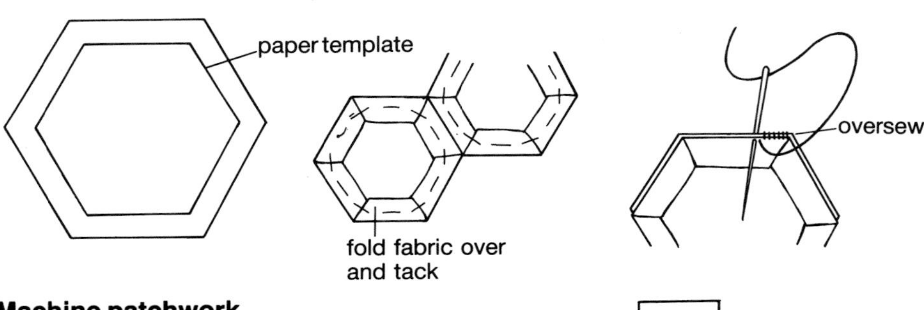

Machine patchwork

Divide the fabric into squares tearing along the grain. (Cut along the cross for triangles.) Machine the squares together into strips. Trim the corners to reduce bulk. Join strips into sheets. Sheets of patchwork can be joined together to make bedspreads, for example.

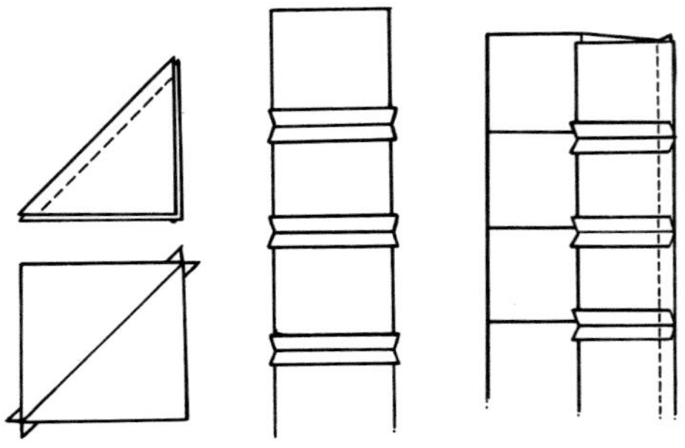

Investigations

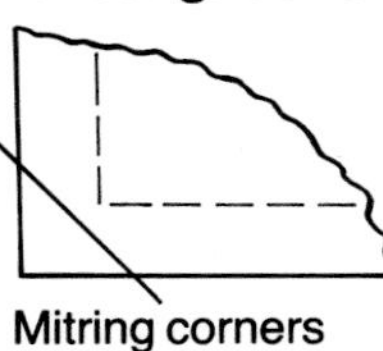
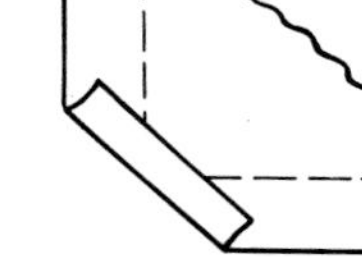
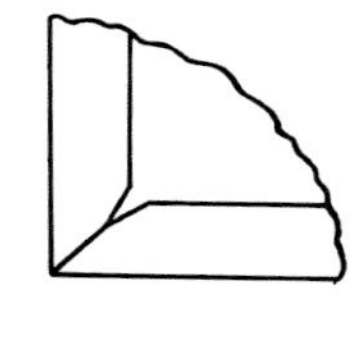
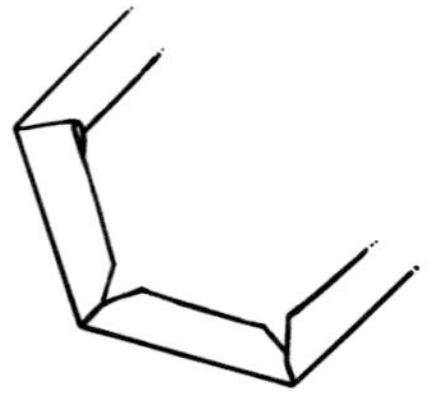

Mitring corners

▲ Cut out a triangle, diamond, square, and hexagon in your chosen fabric.

Using the iron, and the technique of mitring where necessary, make the turnings as shown in the diagram.

On which shapes are the corners easiest and least bulky to turn?

Three dimensional patchwork

Brightly coloured patchwork shapes can be used to make bricks, balls, soft hats, covers, lampshades, and many other three dimensional objects.

▲ Investigate how pentagons and hexagons are assembled to make a football. Draw both shapes in their respective construction circles to have 5 cm sides (p.13). Trace and cut out several thin card circles with the shapes marked inside them. Fold along the edges of the shape. Use the remaining parts of the circle as 'turnings' to staple, pin, or glue together for your mock-up.

Cut out your pentagons and hexagons adding 1 cm turnings to all edges. Combine the hexagons and pentagons to make a football cushion, or a soft ball for a toddler. (Choose a suitable stuffing.)

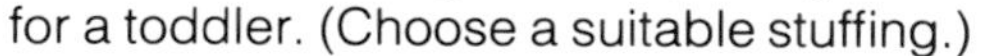

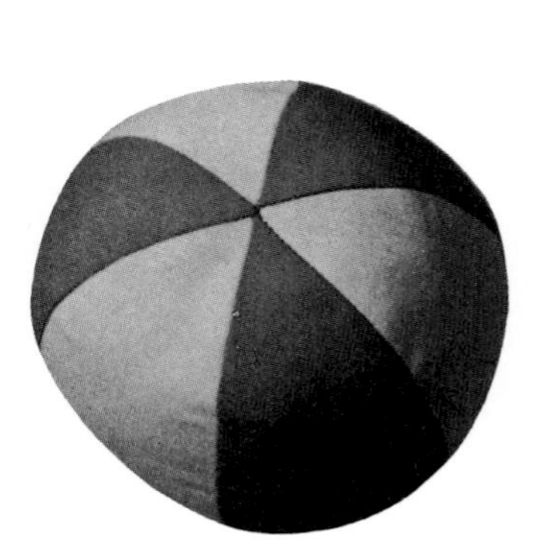

Three dimensional patchwork

▲ Investigate how triangles in circles can be assembled to form a ball. Cut circles from greeting cards with pinking shears. Draw triangles within them. Staple or glue the triangles together by the turnings, and staple a hanging loop into one join.

If you use fabric then a 1 cm seam allowance must be added to each side of the triangle.

▲ Design a patchwork ball, or a lightly stuffed cushion using this idea.
Here are some briefs that can be worked in patchwork and/or appliqué.

▲ Design a cushion using the theme 'crossword' or 'chessboard'.

▲ Make a design using shapes of matching patterned and plain fabric. Use it on an item of your choice.

▲ Using patchwork and appliqué, feature a window design in a picture, bedhead, or duvet cover. Don't forget your plan of action when realizing a brief.

Plan of action

1. Make a sketch of an appliqué picture.
2. Draw up the pattern to full size.
3. Trace off the shapes and cut them out in fabric, allowing for turnings.
4. Assemble figures to be appliquéd on to sections. Tack them on to the sections. Machine.
5. Position and tack sections on to background fabric.
6. Work patchwork pieces.
7. Secure carefully to backing fabric.

Weaving

Look up some weaving techniques in a specialist book in your library and in *All About Fabrics*. Practise weaving on a card or cardboard loom.

A belt loom

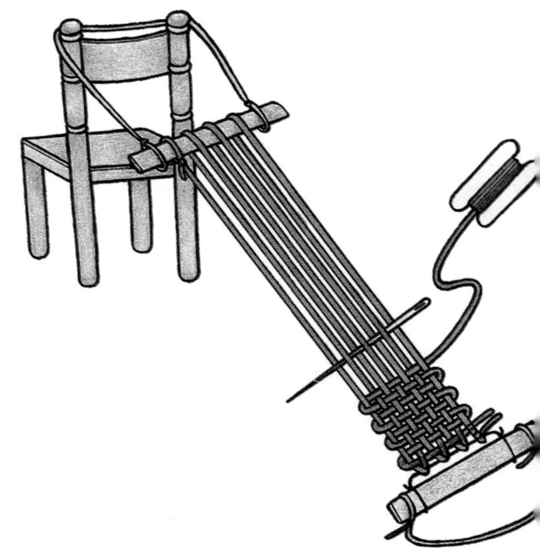

▲ Make a belt, head band, tie, wrist strap, book mark, or guitar strap. A belt loom is simple to make and use.

Method

1 To set it up you need two pieces of flat wood or **dowel rods** about 20 cm long. Tie a piece of cord securely to each end leaving a loop in between, secure this at one end around something static such as a chairback or a door handle. The loop at the other end goes round your waist so that you can sit with the work straight out in front of you keeping both hands free to weave.

2 Decide on the length of the warp and the number of warp threads you want to weave. The warp length will determine the length of the item, including tassels (un-woven warp threads), and the *number* of warp threads will determine the width of the item. As the threads are pulled together during weaving, the length and width will shrink. Allow for about 20% shrinkage when weaving with wool.

If you want to weave to the *end* of the warp threads, e.g. for a tie, wind the warp around some wire and tie the wire on to the dowel rods. The wire can be slipped out when the work is complete, leaving a self-neatened selvedge.

3 **To warp**: place the two end pieces (**rods**) the desired length of the item (plus allowance) apart and parallel to each other. Secure the rods in position with **pegs** and a **peg board**. Tie the end of the warp thread securely to one of the rods and wind the thread from rod to rod until the diagonally opposite corner is reached. Keep the distance between each warp thread consistent.

4 **To weave**: use a **bodkin** to lead the way through the warps. Follow this path with a cardboard shuttle. Slip your fingers between the threads to ease the shuttle through. Ensure even working by patting each woven thread down with a ruler before beginning the next line.

Colour

Attractive patterns can be made by varying the colours of the warp and weft. Experiment with the numbers of warp threads to make stripes and checks.

Finishing

There are several ways to finish the ends:
a make tassels by cutting the warp threads around the rod and knotting in groups of four **b** add beads to the tassels **c** machine the ends with zig-zag and leave a fringe **d** hemstitch by hand.

Tapestry weaving

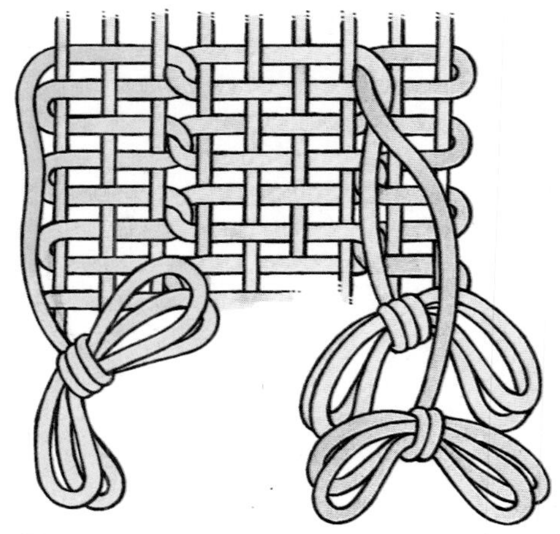

Change colour using vertical interlocking

Beautiful rugs and wall hangings can be made by **tapestry** or **picture weaving**.

In tapestry weaving the weft does not pass from end to end but different colours are wound back and forth along the warp following a preconceived design.

A rectangular wooden frame is used with nails placed at 1 cm intervals along it. The frame is warped with cotton twine, and a separate **flat shuttle** or **tapestry needle** is used for each colour.

To change colour a technique called vertical interlocking is used (see diagram). (There are other techniques – look them up.)

A wide variety of threads can be used, from tapestry wool to velvet, rags, or even plastic.

▲ Plan a simple design in three colours using straight horizontal, vertical, or diagonal lines. Start working it on your frame. Do not follow the design exactly, let the technique lead you. By experimenting in this way you will learn which designs are suitable for tapestry weaving.

Picture weaving

Once the technique of tapestry weaving has been practised, making and developing designs becomes more satisfying.

▲ Design a warm covering for a damp wall.
You might realize this brief by making a thick woven picture.
Make several full size sketches of your design before you begin.
Choose the best sketch and mark the possible material and colour combinations on it. Draw the design in ink on the cotton twine warp. Weave the panel.

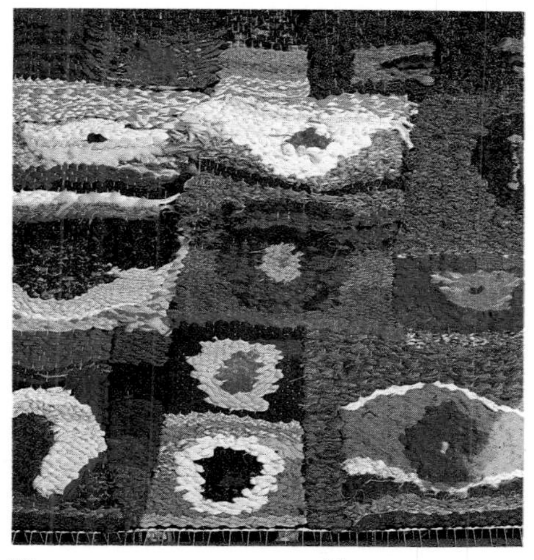

These eyes were woven with rags

Lampshades

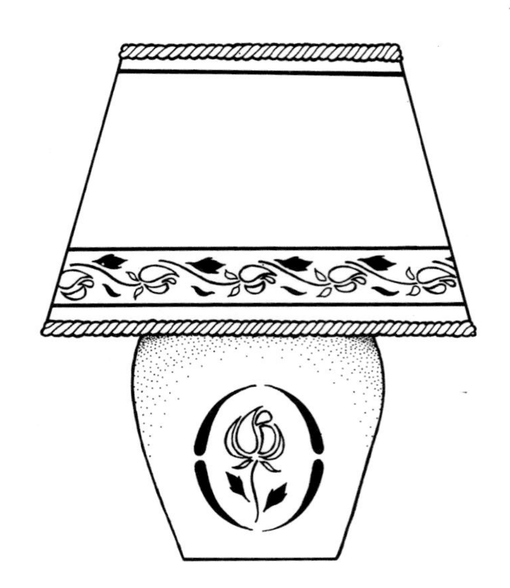

Here are three design briefs:

1. Design and make a shade for a nursery night-light.
2. Using the light from a table lamp, give a welcoming glow to your entrance hall.
3. Design and make a bedside light to shine on a book or clockface.

Before construction of the lampshade can begin, the brief should be fully analysed and possible design solutions investigated.

Investigations

▲ *Shape*

You will need a low power bulb (40 watt) in a room which can be darkened. Make a cone of paper big enough to avoid scorching by the bulb. Cut off the point of the cone at an 8 cm radius. Secure the edges of the cone with sticky tape, staples, or glue.

Investigate the effects of varying the position of the cone around the light. Can you direct the light? When might this be useful?

Make some more shades from different shapes e.g. cones from a quarter circle, a half circle, a three-quarter circle, or even a rectangle. Investigate how the different shapes of cone direct the light and shield the eyes. What is the effect of the wide three-quarter circle saucer shape placed *beneath* the lighted bulb?

Think about the position of the light source in the room. Write up your results and decisions.

▲ *Fabric*

Investigate the effects of holding different fabrics in front of the light. Think about weave, light diffusion, atmosphere, etc., and write up your results.

What effect does using a patterned fabric or a motif have? When would these be suitable?

Colour

The colour of the shade has a great impact so carry out your investigations carefully. Think about the colour scheme of the room and the atmosphere that you want to create, write up your results.

Having looked at how shape, colour, and fabric can achieve your desired effects, look again at the choice of fabric. It must be **practical** and should not scorch or burn, so refer to fabric qualities before making the final selection.

Frame

The whole appearance of the lamp is governed by the shape of frame. Choose one that is in proportion to the stand, is the correct size and shape for the position it will occupy, and one which will cause the light to be directed or diffused as required.

Construction

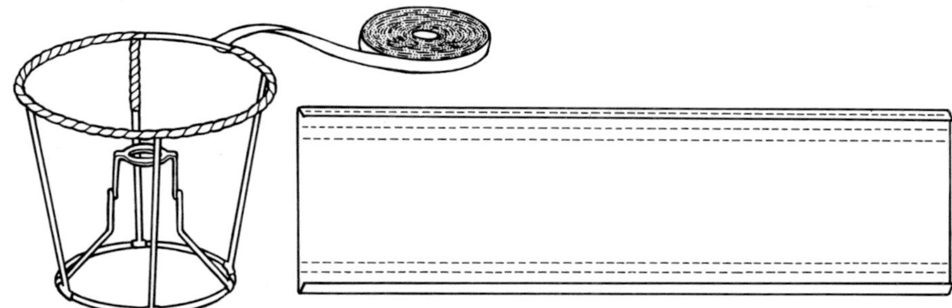

Prepare the frame. Draw up the gathering lines to the size of the shade.

Prepare the frame

Bind the frame very firmly with binding tape of a matching colour so that the fabric can be sewn on to it without the tape slipping or twisting.

Hold the frame upside-down and start on one of the upright struts near the base of the shade. Make a figure of eight around the strut, bandage up a little way to get a firm start, then return to the base and bandage round the circumference, continually overlapping the tape by about half its width. Continue the process, up one strut and down the next. Finally, bind the top circumference, finish with a figure of eight, and sew down the final end.

Cover the frame with fabric

For bucket shapes, choose a fabric with a firm weave that will not stretch. This is important as the seam may then be on the bias grain. Measure the depth and circumference of the frame and cut out the fabric carefully.

Secure the fabric to the tape with pins, placing the join behind a strut. Roll the fabric over the taped frame at the top and bottom, turning in the raw edge. Pin and secure with running stitch. The line of stitching may be covered with braid attached by sewing, or with fabric glue.

Alternatively, the shade may be cut in sections from a pattern and sewn directly on to the tape.

A worked example

For this attractive shade choose a fine fabric. Synthetics are useful as they do not fray.

1. Cut out a strip of the fabric double the circumference of the frame long, and the depth of the frame plus 5 cm deep.
2. Make small double turnings of 0.5 cm and machine along the long edges.
3. Using the machine, make two lines of gathering 0.5 cm apart, 1 cm from each edge.
4. Draw up the gathering lines to the size of the shade. Remember that the bottom is wider than the top.
5. Attach the fabric to the frame, pinning the machine stitched lines securely to the tape and overlapping the ends just slightly to hide the opening.
6. The top and bottom may be further decorated with braid, or embroidery may be worked over the machining.

Lampshades may be lined with a fine fabric to give a professional finish, particularly where the inside is visible. It may be more convenient to attach the lining before the final braiding is done. Fringeing and braid should be of the same type as the fabric in matching or contrasting colours.

Knitting

Before you begin knitting visit a jumble sale. There you can pick up knitted items very cheaply. Unravel them, wash the wool, and use it for your first knitting adventures. Collect oddments of wool from other knitters too. It can *all* be used.

Stocking stitch

Many exciting effects can be achieved with a simple stitch like this one (one row plain, one row purl).

Random colour
Change the colour of your wool as often as you like, and *knit the ends in.* This gives interesting colourful effects.

Odd pins
Use one large pin, say size 7½ (1) and a smaller one, say size 4 (8). This gives a lovely loopy texture that is warm to wear. It grows quickly too!

Textured yarn
Robin Charade wool varies in texture along its length. It is shaggy, fluffy, thick, fine, curled, and lumpy. It knits up to form a very attractive and unusual texture. You can experiment in the same way with wools of different textures, knitting them in at random to see the variety of effects that this produces.

▲ Experiment to find as many designs as possible using stocking stitch.

This scarf was knitted entirely in stocking stitch

Other stitches

Colour
Regular colour patterns can be achieved with stitches like this one:
Knit four rows of stocking stitch. Change colour by tying new wool to the old at the end of a row.
Row 5 Knit 5, slip 1 (put it on the right hand needle without working it). Repeat all the way to the end of the row.
Row 6 Purl slipping the same stitches. Repeat rows 5 and 6
Row 9 Change to another colour or revert to the first one. Knit 2. *Slip 1 knit 5. Repeat from * to the end of the row.
Row 10 As row 9 but purl.
Repeat rows 9 and 10.
Change to another colour and repeat these 8 rows.

Texture
Knitted items have resilience (they spring back into shape). The resilience of the knitting may depend on the stitch used.

Ribbing gives elasticity by producing upright bands drawing the shape up. It is used on cuffs, neck, and waist edges to tighten the shape to fit the body.

With an even number of stitches on the row, knit 1 and purl 1 alternately. Or, with a number of stitches divisible by 4, knit 2 and purl 2 alternately.

It is possible to knit 1 and purl 1 alternately *without* drawing the work up in ribs. To do this always begin the next row with the *same* kind of stitch as you finished the last row with. This is called **moss stitch**. The effect is interesting but flat. Try it and then experiment with other sequences of plain and purl stitches to see what effects you can achieve. Here is one example:

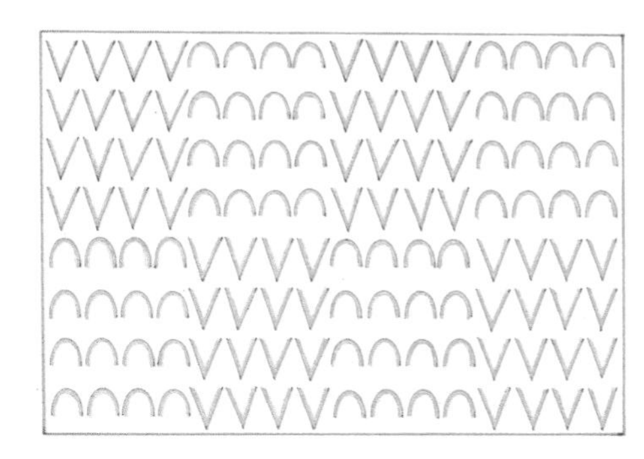

▲ See if you can work out this pattern. Start from right to left on the bottom row. Write down Row 1 Knit 4 purl ——.

Then think of it from the wrong side. Write the whole pattern for the illustration.

▲ Knit and purl stitches at random. This again gives a different but attractive texture.

▲ Make an experimental scarf (40–80 stitches wide) to use as a resource showing as wide a variety of stitches as possible. Experiment with the stitches described, and any others you have learned, on your scarf. Add new stitches as you learn them.

▲ For what purposes other than garments can knitting be used? Think of some ideas and carry one out.

Tassels

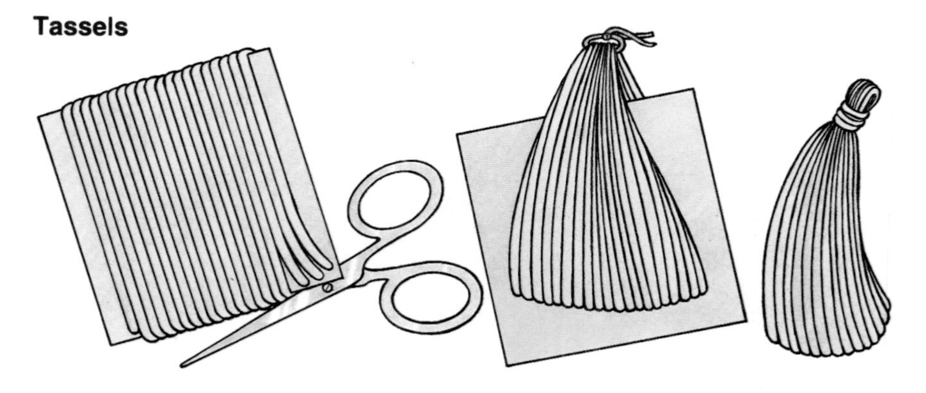

Wind yarn around a card cut to the required length of the tassel. Cut the yarn along one edge and tie a strand around the yarn at the other. Remove the card keeping the threads folded in half, wind yarn tightly around both thicknesses just below the fold. Secure it.

Tassels may be sewn to the edges of scarfs, shawls, or ponchos.

Rugmaking

Rugmaking is done by forming a **pile** with lengths of yarn using a simple **hook** to knot the yarn into a firm base. Pile gives a feeling of warmth and softness. This texture is ideal for a hearth rug, bedroom mat, bath mat, or a wall hanging for a cold room.

Materials

Traditionally wool has been used for rugmaking because it is warm, thick, and resilient. However, nylon and acrylic fibres, with their 'easy-care' qualities, are very suitable for floor coverings. These yarns are particularly useful for bath and toilet mats since they are washable and dry quickly. Colourful fabrics cut into strips are very effective materials for rugmaking. If the fabric is cut on the cross it does not fray. A hard wearing pile makes a good commercial carpet so fabrics like enkalon or acrilan are used for carpets as well as traditional wool.

The chosen material needs to be cut into lengths of about 10 cm. Yarn can be bought in packs ready cut but this is more expensive.

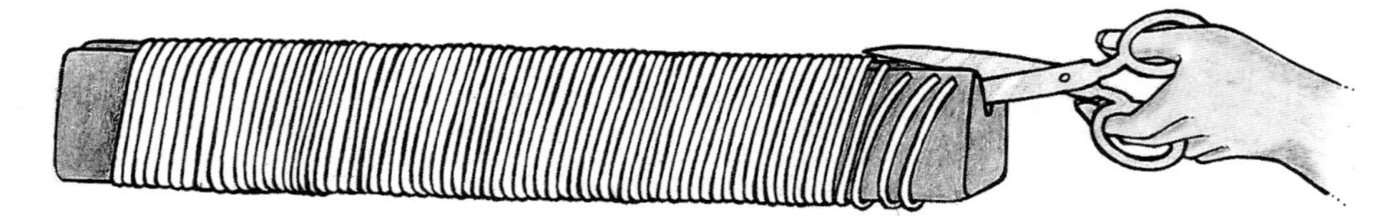

To cut rug yarn wind it around a cutting gauge. This is a strip of wood with a groove along one edge and can be bought or home-made. Cutting along the length of the groove ensures that all the pieces are the same length.

The firm base on to which the pile is worked is usually **grospoint canvas**. This is a firm canvas with threads 0.75 cm apart through which the yarn can be hooked and then knotted.

Method

Rugmaking is done in two simple stages – hooking and tying.

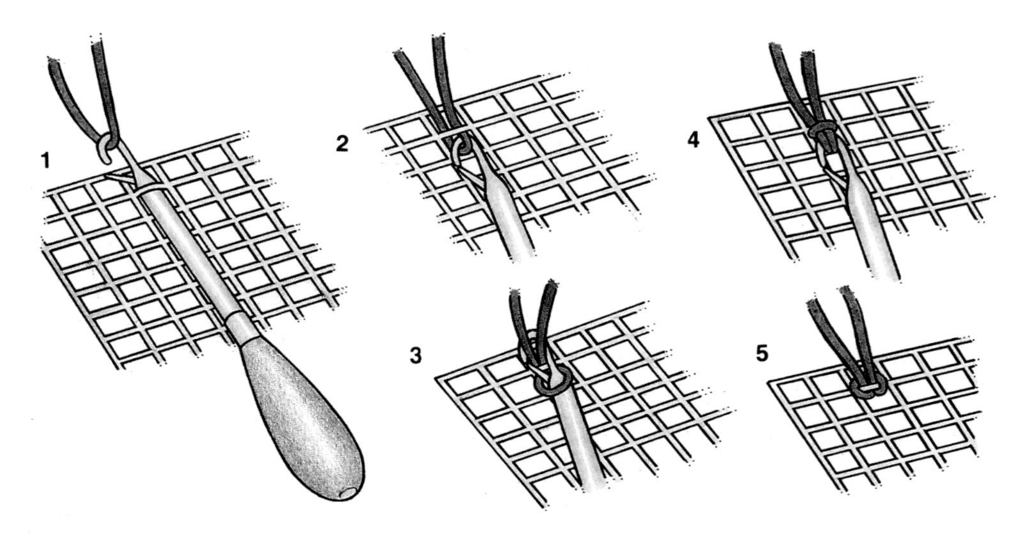

1 Place the hook under a weft thread as shown. With the left hand, place the centre of the yarn in the hook.
2 Draw the hook back until a loop of yarn is formed beneath the weft thread.
3 On the surface, push the hook further through the loop and round the ends of the yarn.
4 Pull the ends of yarn through the loop.
5 Remove the hook and pull the ends with the left hand to secure the loop.

The design

The design can be plotted onto graph paper in the same way as the knitted jumper design (p.32). Count the number of threads on the canvas width and length and, using these figures, plot a graph where each square corresponds to a square of grospoint canvas. Draw your design on the graph paper and colour in the squares. Count the squares of each colour to work out how much yarn of each colour is required.

Enlarging a design
Trace your original sketch onto graph paper and reproduce each line in a 2 mm square into a 1 cm square. This will enlarge your design times five.

How could this design be adapted for rugwork?

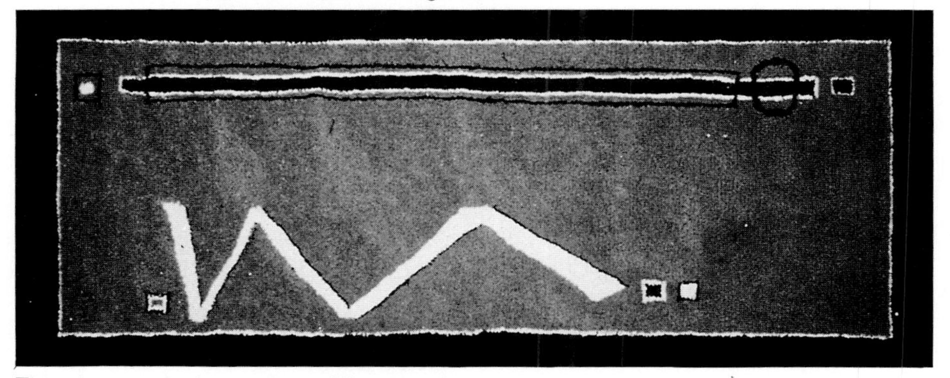

This abstract design works well in rugwork

▲ Design and cost a floor covering for a teenager's room.

Knitting II

Using a pattern

Patterns usually state the number of stitches and rows that should measure 5 cm (2″). Before starting on a project, knit a 5 cm square and make sure that your number of rows is what the pattern expects. If it is not, you can correct the tension by using smaller or larger needles.

Yarn
Yarn varies in thickness. Knitting grows quickly if you use 'double knit' and needles with a large diameter such as size 4½(7) or 4(8). Two-ply or three-ply yarn is finer – only two or three yarns are twisted together. Finer needles such as 3½(10) or 2¾(11) give small neat stitches. Patterns are daintier, picture outlines are more clearly defined, but the knitting grows more slowly.

Patterns offer scope for making plain, shaped, or patterned items. By understanding how they are drawn up on squared paper, you can make your own pictures on body warmers, sweaters, etc., to liven-up plain items.

Making a personalized sweater

Three basic shapes

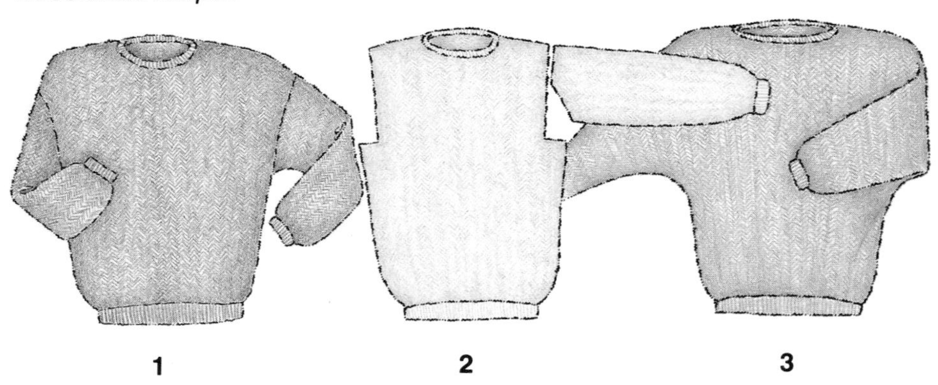

Shape 1 is a rectangle which gives a fashionable dropped shoulder line. The sleeves are attached later. The sleeve is shorter in 1 than in 2, and in 3 it is knitted as part of the whole sweater.
Take the following measurements:

a bust or chest
b length of sweater i.e. from hips to nape of neck
c sleeve length (i) wrist bone to underarm; (ii) wrist bone to shoulder

Decide on the size of needles and number of stitches by looking at a double knit pattern that you have used before.

Knit a 5 cm square with 'double knit' yarn on e.g. size 4 (8) needles. Count the number of rows that you work. Work out the number of rows you need for the length of the sweater.

Take a piece of graph paper and mark the number of stitches along the bottom line and the number of rows up the sides. Draw the basic shape (1, 2, or 3) of the front of the sweater, in proportion, on the graph paper. This is now a scale diagram of your sweater on which you can plot your design.

▲ Design the front of the sweater and plot it carefully onto the graph paper.

Here are three ideas, you will have many more.

1 Use colour and shapes to form an abstract or geometric design (p.12).
2 Use a motif such as a sports figure. Choose a shape which is easily recognizable by simple lines. Avoid too many details as these will not show up well, unless the knitting is quite fine.
3 Draw a simple sketch with the main colour of the sweater forming the background.

When you have drawn your design on graph paper, colour the appropriate squares. Study the effect of your colours and the position of the elements in your design. Now is the time to make minor adjustments or completely redesign.

You are now ready to knit up your design. Remember to allow for the ribbing. Knit this first before starting the pattern. Work with the plan in front of you. Read the pattern of your design from the graph paper *starting at the bottom right hand corner*, the knit row. Read the second, your purl row (and every other even row) *from left to right*. Tick each row as you complete it.

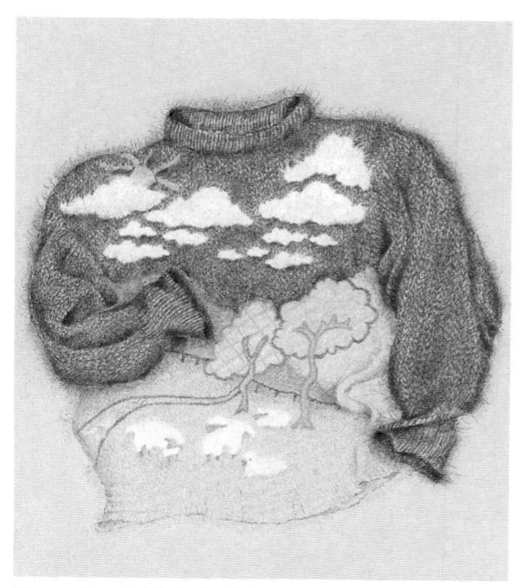

From the initial sketch ...

... to the finished article

More on colour

You can devise your own patterns using colour. Work it out on graph paper first (p.32).

Changing wools
When working coloured shapes or bands twist the two coloured threads together where they meet to make the knitting continuous. Carry the second colour along the back until needed, stranding or weaving it behind the colour being knitted. Hold the colour *not* being used over the forefinger and the little finger of the left hand.

Stranding

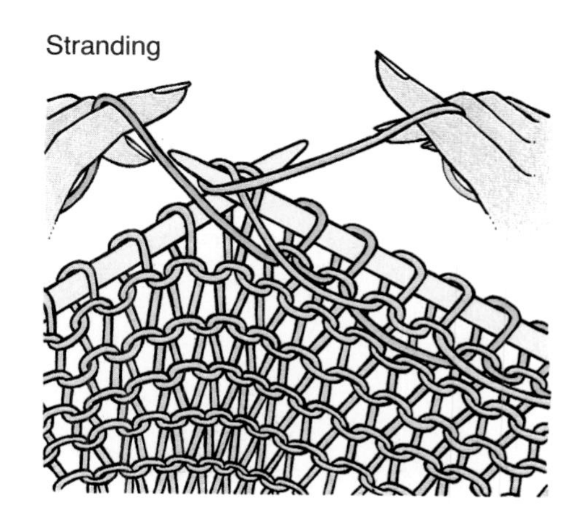

Cut-out work

Cut-out work can be strong and bold or quietly dainty. Both effects add interest to all sorts of creative designs.

Method

All sections to be cut out must be completely surrounded by a firm stitch to prevent fraying. The fabric is then cut away leaving the stitched outline of the design.

Buttonhole stitch forms a strong edge for cut-out work, buttonholes, appliqué, etc. Hold the work in your left hand and insert the needle towards you. Wrap the needle thread around the point. Draw the needle through and then away from you, so that a knot forms on the raw edge.

Machine satin stitching set at, say, length 0.3 and width 4 is also close enough to prevent fabric fraying. It is quicker than buttonhole but needs control to achieve fine work.

The edge produced in these ways is firm enough to cut, even when fine materials are used. You can outline flower shapes, cut them out and make them up for button-holes, or to fix on Valentine cards or box covers. Rosettes in your team's colours can also be made in this way.

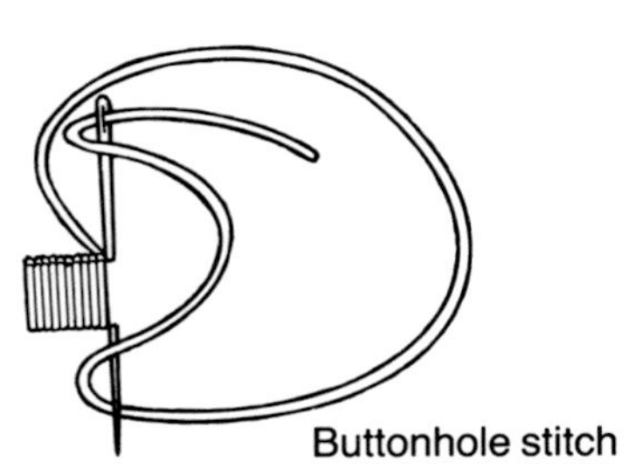

Buttonhole stitch

Satin stitch is often used to decorate cut-out work

An example of cut-out work

▲ Design a Christmas wall panel.

Materials

Light blue or off-white base fabric for sky, 5 cm bigger than picture; yellow fabric for base beneath lantern area; dark fabric for figures, 5 cm bigger than picture; thread matching dark fabric; silver thread for halos and star.

Method

1 Mark out the design on the dark fabric.
2 Machine satin-stitch the outline in matching thread. Satin-stitch by hand the lines of the lantern and along the rays.
3 Cut away the parts completely surrounded by stitching.
4 Lay the cut out work on base fabrics.
5 By hand, satin stitch the halos, anchoring the heads to the fabric beneath.
6 Work the star in satin stitch by hand, or choose a suitable machine stitch.
7 Chain stitch the outlines dividing the figures.

▲ Now form a group and design and make your own 'cut-out' panel.

Questions

1 You have bought two white linen pillowcases at a jumble sale. Make illustrated notes to show how you would turn them into two small attractive tablecloths. Suggest two ways of treating the edges decoratively.

2 Look at the machine stitches on your machine. Say which of the stitches would be suitable for cut-out work, explaining why. Draw them, giving suggestions of how each might be used on adults' clothes, childrens' clothes, or other items.

▲ Using a spider's web for inspiration, design a mat for the centre feature of a bedside table.

▲ Take an old shirt or tee-shirt and make a suitable design on the back for cut-out work. Work the design carefully. Evaluate it. If it is successful, make a garment using cut-out work as the only decorative feature.

Soft toys

The following table shows the analysis and specification of the brief: design a soft toy.

Analysis		Specification of size, shape, and fabric	
Who?	infant: size of hands →	small paws to hold	'furry' pile fabric correct colour correct shape
	learning →	give realism →	
	teenager →	large	
	adult →	as draught excluder →	long thin shape
Why?	infant: friendship →	strokable →	soft pile
	security →	cuddly → soft	warm, soft fabric
	teenager: as a mascot or ornament →	large →	dressed for a game suitable expression
Where?	infant: nursery, bed, pram, floor →	hygienic; →	non-absorbent quick drying
		washable fabric and stuffing →	polyester
	teenager: sports field →	withstand damp, sun, etc. →	synthetics
	bed-sit room →	colour in surroundings →	non flammable: modacrylic; nylon, polyester stuffing
When?	throughout infancy into childhood and longer →	strong →	durable fabric strong seams
	teenager: at sports matches →	safety	
How used?	baby uses mouth to examine →	hygienic; washable fabric →	non-absorbent
		non-toxic paint	
		no sharp points →	safety-lock eyes
	subjected to tough handling in play →	hard wearing fabric →	strong seams and construction

Ask the following questions

What size, shape, colour, texture should the toy be? How should it be constructed? What are the qualities needed? What fabrics have these qualities?

Here are details of some fabrics. You should find more.
Acrylic, **Polyester**, or **Nylon fur fabric** sold by the metre in various colours including black and white.
Gold and brown **modacrylic fur fabric** sold in pieces both spotted and striped. **Curled acrylic** and **modacrylic** in white, black, or grey.
Felt cuts economically, as it has no grain. It is easy to handle and sew, and does not fray. It is easy for children to make their own toys in felt. However, it does absorb water and takes time to dry.
Old coat fabric. Economical, thick, warm texture. **Mohair**, **duffle**, and **camel** have a realistic texture for a camel, donkey, or bear. But they are heavy, absorbent and do not wash well.

Choosing the shape

Many different toy designs can be made from simple shapes. For example, circles are a good start for an octopus, spider, ladybird, or fantasy creatures.

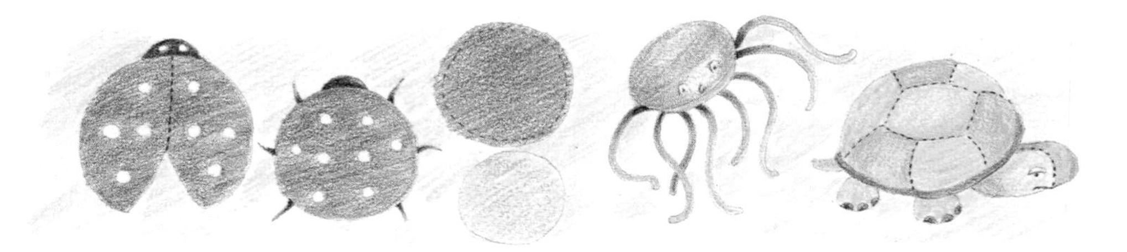

Always keep the basic shape simple. Think of the animal's chief characteristics: the big sad eyes of a white seal, the eight bendy legs of an octopus, a rabbit's long ears, the squirrel's bushy tail, the neck of the giraffe, the crocodile's teeth, and the plump duck's large webbed feet.

Using these characteristics draw a shape, side view. Two sides give two dimensions, and this is all that is required for some toys. To add a third dimension, draw a gusset (a strip) to go down the front and underneath. Make the gusset wider where the animal is broader e.g. the duck's breast, the bull's shoulder, the kangaroo's pouch. Keep simplifying your design.

The animal will stand or sit well if it is broader at the base. A wider spread of weight at the bottom, i.e. a low centre of gravity, makes it stand firm and also makes it difficult to knock over. Features such as flat webbed feet, a mouse's ears, or a donkey's tail are added afterwards. (They will be sewn into the seams where possible.)

Colour can give a toy character, e.g. red looks strong and bold, pastel colours look young, and white can show innocence.

To give realism to the nose, use shiny black fabric such as satin or taffeta, or embroider closely in satin stitch with shiny black thread. Alternatively safety lock noses can be bought to fix on.

Soft Toys II

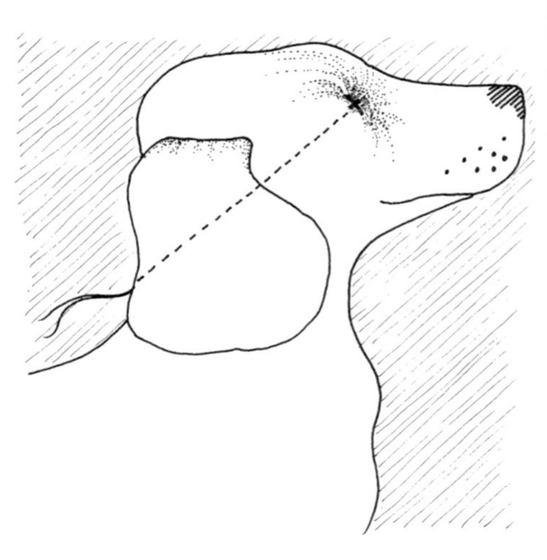

Always check the position of the eyes before stitching

Eyes

The eyes and mouth really give character and show emotion. You can make your animal (or doll) look surprised, funny, sad, puzzled, cheeky, or cross simply by the position of eyes and mouth, and the stitches used. Eyes should be set well into the head, except with amphibians like frogs. Check the position of the eyes by making stitches on the wrong side in buttonhole thread, drawing them to the back of the neck. This ensures a lifelike position.

Eyes can be made of coloured felt with large pupils. Where appropriate embroider lashes on. These embroidered or felt eyes look best on home-designed toys. Check their effect as you position them after stuffing the toy.

Buttons, beads, or ready made eyes must be securely fixed with a strong button thread so that they *cannot be removed.* If a child swallows one, the consequences can be very severe indeed.

Safety-lock plastic eyes have good expressions. They must be fixed through fabric with a special tool, and secured with a safety lock. They are permanent, so check the position of eyes carefully before fixing them. On a bought pattern you may have the eye position marked. It is easier to fix it *before* sewing the pattern piece. If a fabric has any degree of stretch put a stick-on patch or a piece of vilene on the inside to provide a firm base.

Making the pattern

If you have drawn your own shape, draw 1 cm round your pieces to allow for turnings. Cut out your pattern in paper. Pin it together (or use blu-tac to hold it) and check it for shape, position of wings, ears, eyes, etc. When you are satisfied with your design, cut it out in card. Label each piece clearly saying what it is, and which is the nose and tail end of it. Card gives a firmer outline to cut round when using knitted-backed fur or thick fabric.

To cut out

1. Place the pattern on the fabric so that the straight grain goes from nose to tail. The pile must stroke the same way as the animal's fur would stroke.
2. Fit the pieces on closely together so that no fabric is wasted. (Felt has no grain, so pieces can be fitted on even more economically, like a jigsaw.)
3. Pin fur fabric very securely as the knitted backing fabric stretches.
4. Cut out carefully. Unpin the pieces, but keep the pattern piece on the fabric until you actually sew it. This avoids confusion. Seams can be made on the right side if you are using felt. Sew other seams on the wrong side using straight stitch, swing needle, or over-lock (look in your machine instruction book). The ears and tail are more securely fixed if they are sewn *into* a seam. Leave an opening in a central place, through which you can push stuffing to all parts. Soft toy shapes can be put to good use in the home.

▲ Say what qualities you would need in the fabric for the following items. In each case plan the design for the item stating the approximate size, fabric, and other material needed, and the details of making. Draw the finished results.

- **a** an attractive draught excluder in the shape of a dachshund, caterpillar, worm, or snake
- **b** on octopus pyjama case
- **c** a pouffe or footstool in the shape of a tortoise.

Stuffing

For good results stuffing should be light, washable, and very well packed.

Polyester filling absorbs no water. It is light and resilient. This means it is easily washable, dries quickly, and springs back into shape immediately. Soft toys can thus be machine washed without losing their shape. The qualities of both stuffing and material should be considered when washing toys.

Cut-up old **nylon tights** make an economical stuffing. The fabric is light, washable, and dries quickly. It shapes well if packed tightly.

Stuffings suitable for ornamental toys only

Kapok is light, fluffy, and gives a good shape. However it is absorbent. Therefore it is unsuitable for washable toys. It goes lumpy and takes a long time to dry. Toys thus lose their shape. It was widely used for toys and cushions before polyester became available. (The zip-on outer cushion covers were washed separately.) **Foam chips** or **shreddies** are useful to fill up the *centre* of a bulky toy. However, they are messy to use and can give a lumpy effect. **Wood wool** is a residue from wood, sometimes used in bought toys. It is not as light nor as effective as polyester for stuffing.

Filling your toy

When filling, put a large cloth on your worktable to fold up after use or you will find the stuffing everywhere. Wear an apron. Keep the stuffing in its bag, or work with it in an old pillowcase. When you want some, fluff it up with a fork and push it to the furthest parts of the animal first, using a wooden spoon handle as a pusher. Push as much stuffing into the furthest parts as you can. **Do not leave any spaces**. If the stuffing is not packed tightly enough the shape of the toy will change. Be careful to make limbs stout and firm, or they will wobble.

Stuffing gives shape and realism to the toy, so time and effort spent on this stage is well worth it. When you can put no more stuffing in leave the toy overnight to settle, then try to put your fingers in again. Pack it more tightly.

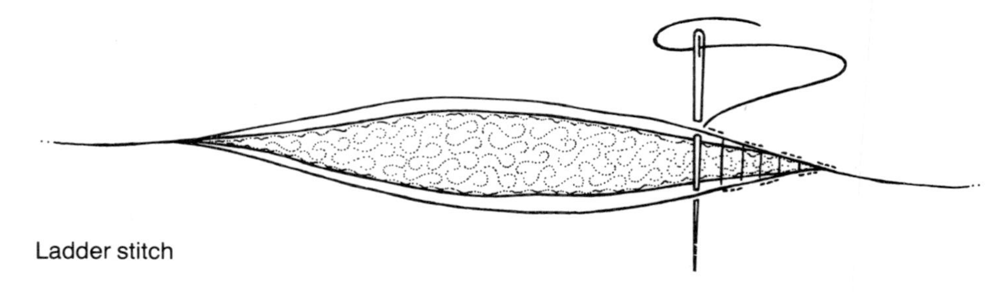

Ladder stitch

Close the join with **ladder stitch** worked with strong matching button thread, on the right side. The stitch turns the raw edges in as well as closing the gap. Fasten off very securely with backstitches.

Making dolls

Making dolls can be satisfying and fun, expecially if care is taken when dressing them.

Method

Carry out the usual analysis and specification to come up with the best fabric, size, and shape. Remember that the chosen fabric needs to be strong enough to hold the tightly packed stuffing.

1. Make a drawing of a doll on graph paper and enlarge to the appropriate size (p.32).
2. Cut out the design in strong card.
3. Pin the card on to the fabric (folded over) and cut around it.
4. Sew the fabric pieces wrong sides together leaving a 10 cm opening in the side for stuffing. (Double-sew for extra strength.)
5. Trim the tight curves, e.g. between the legs, to ease turning to the right side.
6. Turn to the right side and stuff. Start by stuffing the hands, then the arms, then the feet and legs, then the head, and lastly the body. Ladder stitch the opening (p.67).

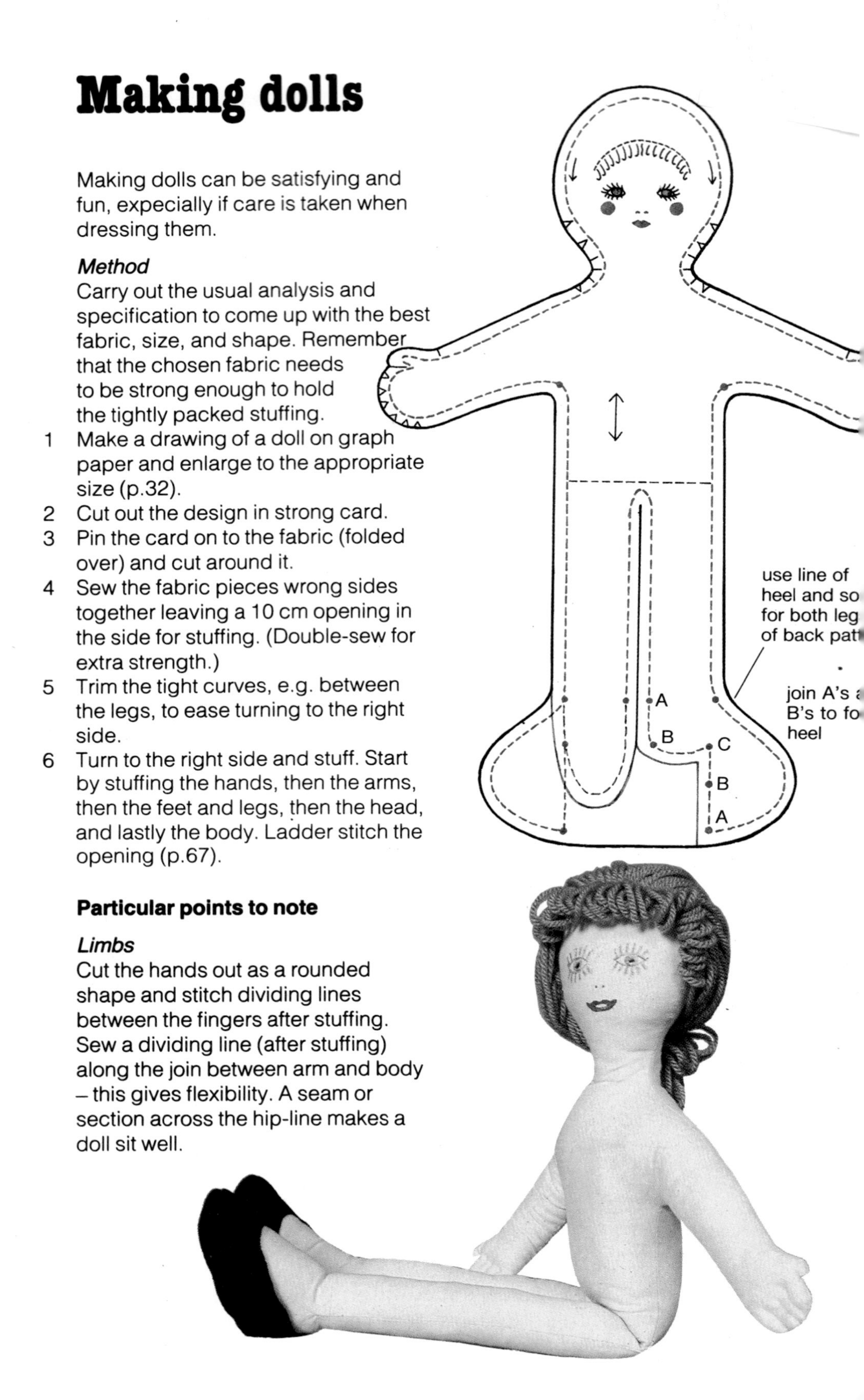

Particular points to note

Limbs

Cut the hands out as a rounded shape and stitch dividing lines between the fingers after stuffing. Sew a dividing line (after stuffing) along the join between arm and body – this gives flexibility. A seam or section across the hip-line makes a doll sit well.

Faces
Ready-made faces can be bought in craft shops and stuck on. But it is much more interesting to design your own. Experiment with fabric paints and crayons and emphasize features using embroidery. Think about the expression on the doll's face, this gives it character.

Hair
Experiment with wool, pieces of fabric, brillo pads, thick yarn, plastic, and anything else you can think of. Use scarfs, hats, ribbons, and bands to add character.

To make a parting wind wool along a piece of card and machine along the centre line. Fix to the scalp by stitching along the parting.

A fringe can be made by winding wool around a piece of fabric and placing it above the face.

Curly hair is formed by making long loopy stitches with wool, using a darning needle. Lots of stitches are needed for a good effect.

Dolls' clothes
The first thing to remember is that small items are more tricky to sew than large ones, so keep the design simple!

Study history books for ideas on designing historical clothes. These look more genuine when hand sewn and made in natural fibres.

Finishing touches

Time spent in finishing and presenting an item is always worthwhile.

Braids and bindings

Binding and braids and other trimming, decorate and give individuality to clothes and household items. A braid that is compatible with the fabric for wash and wear should be chosen. Braid may be attached by straight stitch, swing needle, or machine embroidery stitch.

It is always easier to do any decorative work whilst the fabric is flat (p.34).

Look at this example of a realization of the brief: 'Design and make a casual carrier bag'.

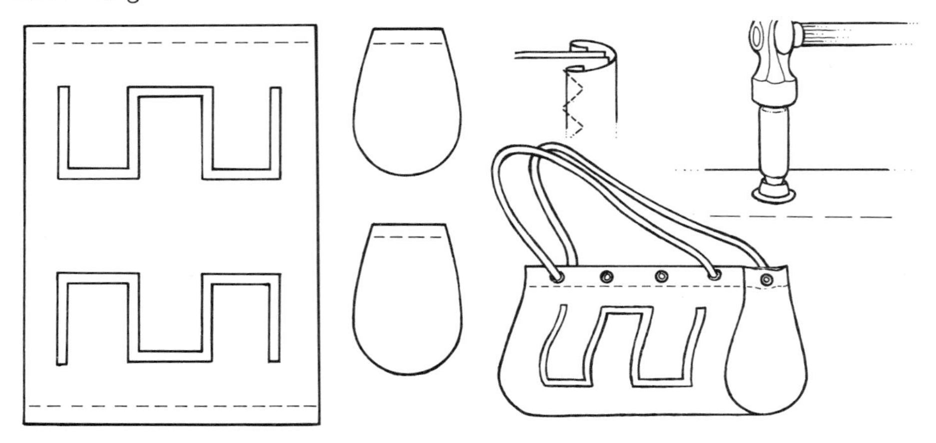

1. Cut out the fabric and decorate with braid.
2. Join seams: either wrong sides together with binding using 3 step zig-zag or, right sides together as shown.
3. Turn down top edge. Stamp eyelet holes using a bought applicator. Thread cord through.

This bag may be stiffened with card or plastic; lined or piped. The simple and quick decoration of the bag gives an excellent effect.

Simple bead work

The application of beads onto fabric is quick and easy, adding colour, texture, and sparkle to the work.
Beads are particularly effective when used to emphasize long flowing lines.
For this work the beads can be threaded up, laid on the surface of the work and oversewn at intervals with fine matching thread.
If beads are to be applied individually, a base fabric with a visible thread should be used.

Drawn thread work

A straight hem can be worked decoratively on fabric with even but clearly visible threads, by drawing some. This is called **hemstitching**. Where a panel is worked without a hem it is called **drawn thread work**. Hemstitching in contrasting thread is a good way of finishing off a wall hanging, for example.

Preparation for hemstitching

1. Mark the fabric with a pin at twice the depth of the hem plus a turning.
2. Pick up the single marked thread with a pin. Draw it along the fabric and pull it out. Once the first thread is out, they become successively easier to remove.
3. Remove a panel of say 4–5 mm to give a reasonable depth to work on. The number of threads depends on the texture of the fabric.
4. Fold the double turning of the hem so that the fold comes to the lower edge of the panel.
5. Mitre the corners. Tack in place.

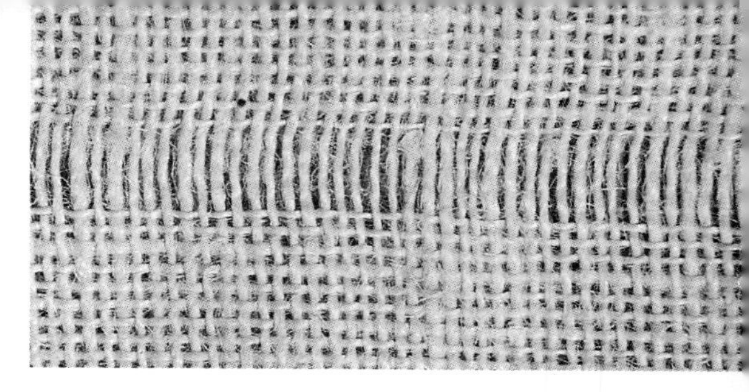

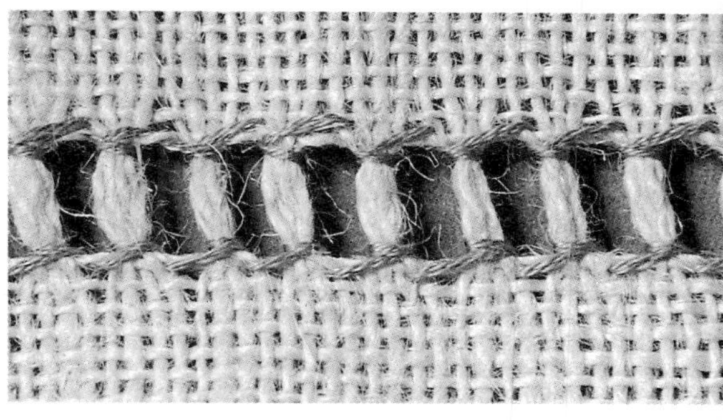

Hemstitching

To hemstitch

Hold the work with the hem nearest to you. Start the thread securely and bring it out on the edge of the hem on the wrong side.

1. Pick up a group of threads (4 or 6) with the needle.
2. Make a stitch downwards into the hem. Then make the next stitch as before, counting the same number of threads in the group each time. Progress from left to right.
3. Work the opposite edge by turning the fabric the other way up.
4. A straight bar is formed if the stitches are worked with the same threads. If an equal number of threads are taken from each group a criss-cross effect is produced. Straight bars can be twisted in centre by weaving a straight thread through.

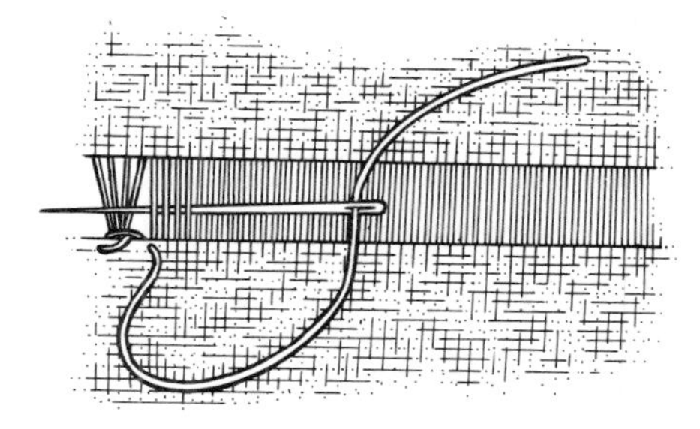

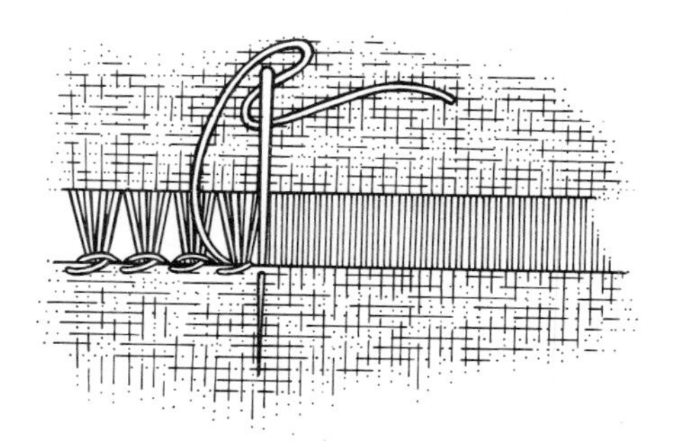

Drawn thread work can be worked with contrasting thread on the right side so that the coloured stitch draws the eye to the panel.

Finishing, mounting, and framing

A neat, strong finish is very important in decorative work. Pressing done correctly at each stage during construction positions fabrics more firmly, and makes working easier and quicker. Attention to these details gives a good professional finish to your work.

Embroidery

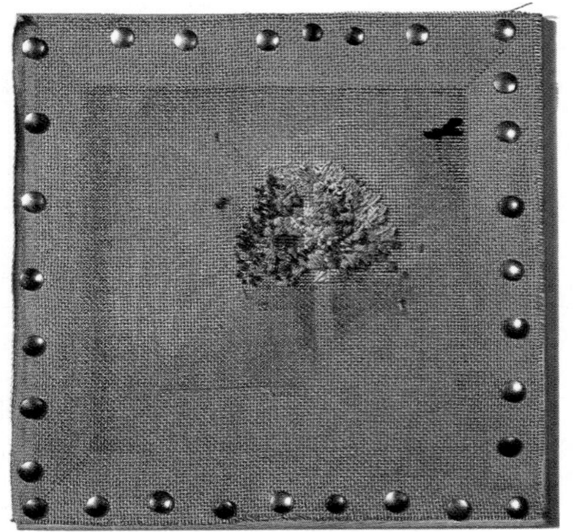

Blocking up

Framing for effect

Embroidery stands out well if it is pressed on the **wrong** side with a damp cloth over a blanket base. The iron removes any creases from the fabric while the embroidery sinks into the soft blanket. Ensure that the fabric is ironed till dry or it will crumple again.

Blocking or squaring up

When fabric is *covered* with embroidery such as needlepoint, the fabric may need squaring up to correct pulling. This is particularly important to ensure a flat finish when framing.

Dampen the fabric with a flower spray, or fine flour dredger, so that it responds to pulling. Lay it on a right-angled squared board and pull into position. Check the right-angles with a set square. Starting at one corner, and using rust free tacks, pin the fabric at 2 cm intervals up the two adjacent sides. Pull hard and pin, squaring up until it is all pinned on. Leave overnight to dry completely.

Knitting

Before joining up knitted items press the pieces (especially stocking stitch as this tends to curl). Use a cool dry iron for synthetic yarns and a damp cloth and warm iron for wool. Do not press ribbing.

Join up knitted items by hand, using the same yarn. Straight machine stitching stretches the seams, so machine as for stretch fabric.

Weaving

If you weave fabric to make a comb case or spectacle case there is no need for turnings as a selvedge is already woven (that is a self neatened edge). The woven fabric should simply be folded in half and the join oversewn neatly.

The lining for, say, a spectacle case should be made separately. It should be made 1 mm smaller than the article in a toning backing fabric. The lining should be placed, right side showing, inside the case and hemmed neatly 1 mm below the opening.

Framing

Method

You will need a **frame**, **board** and **cardboard** to fit in the frame exactly, a sheet of brown paper, and some panel pins.

1. Press or block the work well to finish it. Light falling on glass emphasizes any unevenness.
2. Lay the work over a wooden backing board or cardboard, pulling taut to flatten it. Secure it on the back with panel pins folding the corners carefully.
3. Sew the fabric from top to bottom and side to side to hold it taut. Remove the panel pins.
4. Place the picture in the frame and place the backing card or board behind it.
5. Fasten the work flat to the backing board using small panel pins or **sprigs**.
6. Glue brown paper over the back including the frame. When the glue is set, trim the edges of the paper.

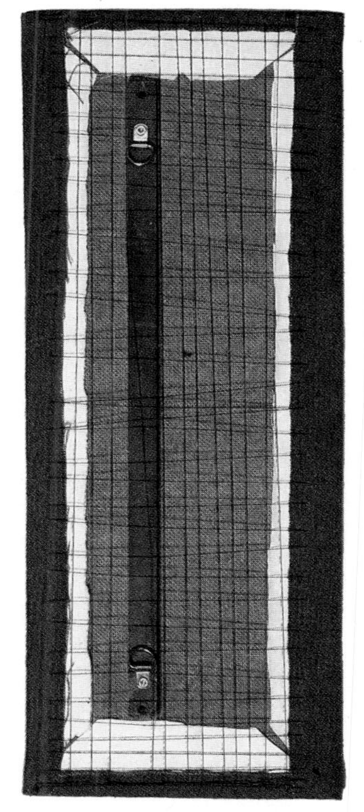

One of the most attractive features of textile work is its interesting texture. So, unless it is very uniform, there is usually no point in putting such work behind glass. However, glass prevents people from touching. Notice how valuable antique lace or embroidery is mounted in a museum. Why is this done?

To mount without a frame

Stretch the work over a backing board and treat as for framing (steps 2 and 3). Staple or glue cardboard to the back securely. Fix adhesive hangers.

Questions

1 Look at a piece of decorative work that you have recently completed. List the factors to be taken into account when framing.

2 What does 'squaring up' mean?

▲ Mount and frame a completed decorative panel. Evaluate it. Do you think it looks any better framed?

PART III

Part III gives examples of how briefs may be realized using various techniques.

Worked briefs

Brief: design a sports bag.

Analysis

Who?	Why?	When?	Where?	How used?
Footballer	to carry rugby/ soccer boots, towel, shirt, etc.	to matches and training sessions regularly in winter	at some distance by bus, or by bicycle	exposed to elements, dirt, heavy weight; hung in locker room
Tennis player	pumps, towel, racket, balls	occasional games in summer		kept in fairly clean conditions

Specification
What qualities are needed?
A strong substantial material unharmed by damp or sunlight.
A secure comfortable carrying handle (for cycling use two shoulder straps to wear 'knapsack style').
A design large enough to carry a towel and all the necessary equipment and clothes.

Investigations

1 Assess size and weight of contents by measurement. Sketch proposed shape.
2 Select fabric and *try out* alternatives. For example, heavy-weight nylon with three step zig-zag edges; nylon backed PVC/leatherette with seams taped or clipped; sailcloth, canvas, and denim (but these do fade in strong sunlight).
3 Estimate size (e.g. 40 cm × 25 cm × 15 cm).
Draw the layout on paper to give minimum number of seams. Add 1.5 cm to *all* edges. Calculate the amount of fabric required.
Calculate the amount of piping cord and binding if used (approximately the perimeter of top plus 5 cm).

Plan of action

1. Cut out.
2. Join strap, put join underneath and sew straps to fabric all round.
3. Work name on pocket.
4. Construct pockets and attach to outside (or inside).
5. Make side seams and press open and neaten with zig-zag, or neaten turnings together and turn towards centre.
6. Join two sections of top, 3 cm at either end. Insert closed zip into position, leaving zip partway open.
7. Position top (right sides together) with sides of bag, matching corner dots with seams. Insert piping if used.
8. Attach top with bag upside down on machine. The top lays flat on the machine bed. Neaten seams then turn the bag right way out.

Brief: design a body warmer.

Analysis

Who?	Why?	When?	Where?	How used?
Old person	to retain body heat for warmth	continually during cold weather	mainly indoors	over indoor clothes for sitting and working about the house
Young person	for warmth outdoors	for walking, snowballing, etc.	outdoors therefore showerproof	over indoor clothes for activities

Specification

A garment which will fit over normal indoor clothes, in a textile which will retain body heat by trapping air in its structure.
Which textile has the required warmth? What size and shape would be suitable? There will be more than one possible design solution. Discussion with your classmates might help here.

Possible solutions

a Quilted fabric with polyester padding. Not too bulky for indoors. Close-weave nylon or polyester which can be showerproof. More bulk should be added for outdoor wear.

b Wool – crimps in fibres and their covering of tiny scales keep fibres apart and trap air. Wool therefore retains body heat.

c Synthetic fibres (acrylics) are bulked. This makes them warmer to handle. Air spaces are created by the structure of knitting or crochet, so clothes made by these methods are particularly warm to wear.

Take appropriate measurements. Draw the design on graph paper, shading in colours of the design.

Make a plan of action, work through the design process flowchart and, if it works, make up the item. Don't forget that <u>you</u> will wear it!

Worked briefs II

Brief: design a wall hanging for a doctor or dentist's waiting room.

Analysis

Who?	Why?	When?	Where?	How used?
Patients	to divert mind from impending visit to doctor or dentist	about 10–20 minutes waiting time at irregular intervals	**a** on sunny wall **b** in drab room	to look at and work out flat on wall
Children			**c** low down on wall	to run fingers along

Specification

What qualities are needed? (These should be listed more fully than in this example.)

One idea would be to make an interesting picture or puzzle to attract attention for about 10 minutes. If you decide to make a maze then choose a striped fabric.

The choice of fabric must meet the specification.

For **a** resistant to sun – acrylic

For **b** bright colours – cotton or acrylic

For **c** washable or wipeable – PVC or plastic

Design: Large square kept flat by dowel rods through top and bottom hems and hung by cord.

Investigation

Try out a maze on squared paper making stripes with a thick felt pen. Cut, arrange, and glue down sections to practise matching stripes. Make a route through, using *Tipp-Ex* to represent the path connecting the stripe trail. Lay some false trails leading nowhere. Try out your puzzle on friends. Adapt it if necessary.

Compare the width of stripes in the fabric to the size of wall hanging. Relate them to the difficulty of the puzzle. Use narrow stripes for a small puzzle and broader stripes for a larger one.

Consider size: 90 cm square or 115 cm square of fabric, allowing a 3 cm hem on all sides. Select about 2 m of matching tape or ribbon, and cord for hanging.

Experiment to find the best size of the maze. Make sure it's visible from the required distance.

The diagram above shows how a maze has been constructed from striped material. Can you work out how is has been made?

Plan of work

1 Starting and ending with a *white* stripe on each edge, cut the fabric into four squares. Cut two along the diagonal in opposite directions. Match the stripes on the cross seam. Join up.
2 Lay quarters together matching stripes. Join sections.
3 Turn 3 cm hems (0.75 then 2.25) on two sides. Machine.
4 Cut braid pieces. Turn under raw edge and machine braid into position.
5 Thread dowel rod through top and bottom hem, leaving ends out. Attach cord to hang up.

Brief: design something for a three year old's birthday.

Analysis and specification

Who?	To assist educational and physical development of child.
Why?	To appeal to sense of sight and touch.
When?	Daytime or bedtime: story in rag book, nursery lampshade, nightlight, or quilt cover.
Where?	Nursery: consider safety with small inquisitive hands.
How used?	Well handled. Realistic texture, shape, and colour increase recognition and help learning.

Here are four examples of how this brief might be realized.

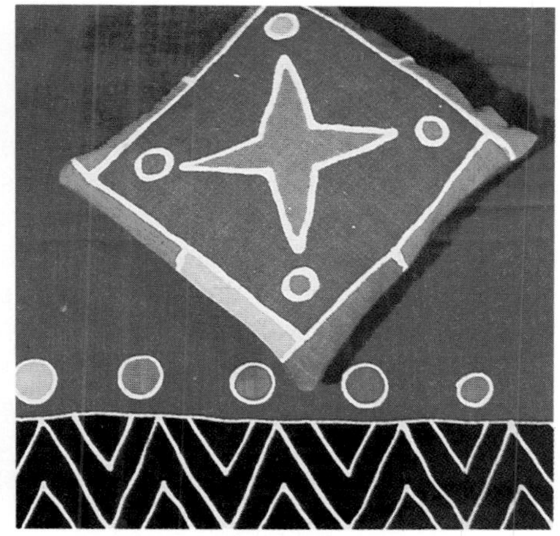

A fabric-painted duvet cover (above)
An embroidered panel (below left)
A textured panel (above left)
A nursery rhyme cushion (below)

Unworked briefs

Here are a selection of briefs from which you can choose particular projects for realizing (making up).

Although the briefs are grouped together in themes, all of them involve a relationship with people or family, home or environment, and sometimes food.

Before you begin, look back at the introduction and make a list of the factors that need to be considered when realizing *all* briefs.

Health and safety

1 Why do cyclists sometimes wear a brightly coloured slipover tabard? Analyse and write the specification for such an item. Make a sketch giving approximate sizes. Make up and evaluate your design.

2 Each winter many housebound elderly people, trying to keep heating bills low, die of hypothermia. Design a body warmer for wear around the house.

3 Design and make an attractive footwarmer as a present for a housebound invalid.

4 Design and make an item which provides a reassuring texture to a young child before falling asleep.

Consumer choice

5 Plan, make, and evaluate an item of your choice to illustrate the scope and versatility of your sewing machine.

6 Evaluate the use of the iron in textile work by making an item in which it plays an important part at several stages.

7 Evaluate forms of nylon for nightwear. Show the versatility of your sewing machine by making and decorating an item of nightwear made in a suitable form of nylon. Say why you have chosen this fabric.

8 Design a wall covering for a community centre.

9 What sort of household article could a beginner make entirely with a sewing machine? Sketch a suitable article and label the diagram to show any special processes made possible by your choice of sewing machine for the beginner. Make up and evaluate your choice. (LEAG.)

10 Texture can be introduced into fabrics in three main ways: yarn type, construction, finish. Suggest how and why the texture produced in *each* way can be used to good effect in garments and household articles for households with different cultural traditions. Relate your suggestions, where appropriate, to food, family, and home.

Sketch an item of clothing or household furnishing which has an interesting texture, and briefly evaluate its aesthetic qualities. Make it up and complete a final evaluation of it. (LEAG.)

Efficiency

11 Design a bag in which to carry a large polythene food box and other items, to and from home economics lessons. (Hint: the food should be carried flat.)

12 Design a packed lunch container to hold polythene boxes, fruit, and an upright bottle or flask. The design should be easily carried, hang from a peg or the back of a chair, and feature the owner's name clearly.

13 Design a cover for a large vessel in which hot soup is carried to a Youth Club.

Using specific techniques

14 Design a bookmark featuring a herringbone weave, and tassels on one end. Draw the bookmark on squared paper giving a suggested size. Suggest two methods of weaving it. Carry out one and evaluate your design in use.

15 Look at a piece of tartan fabric. Work out how the pattern is formed. Draw it on squared paper. Design a set of mats to use beneath a jug and glasses featuring this type of design.

16 Design and weave a set of drinks mats, a comb case, a spectacle case. Evaluate your choice of shape and yarn.

Aesthetic

17 Design and make an emblem for one of your local sports teams.

Home and Community

18 Design and make a reading lamp.

19 Using animals as a theme, design a draught excluder for the door. Evaluate your design's function and aesthetic qualities.

20 What factors would you consider when planning and making a decorative feature for the wall facing the sun in a light room. What qualities would be required in the fabric and decorative material used for curtains in a sunny lounge window? Design, make, and evaluate one of these items.

21 Animals, like humans, need warmth and comfort. For the RSPCA, an animal sanctuary, or your own pet, utilise pieces of yarn or fabric to make a base for a dog basket, a donkey blanket, or a night cover for a parrot cage.

Index